L O S E
WEIGHT
→THROUGH
GREAT SEX
★★★★WITH
CELEBRITIES!

(the Elvis way)

COLIN

McENROE

DOUBLEDAY

NEW YORK LONDON TORONTO SYDNEY AUCKLAND

LOSE

WEIGHT

→ **THROUGH**

GREAT SEX

★★★★ WITH

(the Elvis way)

PUBLISHED BY DOUBLEDAY

a division of Bantam Doubleday Dell Publishing Group, Inc.
666 Fifth Avenue, New York, New York 10103

DOUBLEDAY and the portrayal of an anchor
with a dolphin are trademarks of Doubleday,
a division of Bantam Doubleday Dell Publishing
Group, Inc.

Some of the material in this book appeared previously in the
Hartford Courant and is used under license granted by the
Hartford Courant Co.

Library of Congress Cataloging-in-Publication-Data
applied for

Dedicated to my mother and father,
who really put me on the map.

Acknowledgments

Number one, I'd like to thank Joyce Carol Oates for everything. You're the best, Joyce (Carol).

Also, my sweet wife Thona, David Sperling, M.D., Esther Newberg, Casey Fuetsch (Winner, PEN Award, most consecutive consonants), Herman Gollob, Jim Fitzgerald (hey, where'd he go?), Roy the dog, Roy the Blount. Also, David Epstein. We'll both miss your dad a lot this time around, David. Finally, Garret Condon, Steve Metcalf, Frank Rizzo, David Jacobson, Carole Goldberg, Stef Summers, Mary Feeney, Don D'Elia, Bob Krieger and a bunch of other people at the *Hartford Courant.*

Actually, I don't know Joyce Carol Oates, but I'm figuring some people won't read down this far and will be impressed.

Introduction

I'm sorry about the title.

We went right down to the wire on a choice between this one and *Anna Karenina, Part II,* but in the long run, nobody felt up to hashing things out with the Tolstoi family lawyers.

So I sit here, hankering, gross, mystical, nude and poised to write a self-help book, and I wonder: Would *Hankering, Gross, Mystical, Nude* have been a better title? How about if I dropped *Mystical?*

Well, you can't second-guess yourself forever. When people ask me why I wrote this book, I tell them it's because I believe it's time that somebody stood up and spoke the truth, because they don't teach values in the schools anymore and because I needed, in order to satisfy certain obligations incurred at my local jai alai fronton, the kind of pecuniary assistance that only a large, unfeeling American corporation such as Wedtech or Doubleday could provide.

"Jai alai," for those of you who don't know, is a

Basque phrase meaning "senseless velocity." Jai alai is one of the three official state sports of Connecticut (where I live), the other two being cockfighting and a golf tournament named after Sammy Davis, Jr., one of the original signers of the Constitution.

Cockfighting, while we're on the subject, is a sport with a bad reputation, primarily because most people don't understand what it entails. Here's the truth. In cockfighting, two chickens, wearing spurs, fight to the death while grown men and women wager money.

There. You see? Armed with the truth, you can see that cockfighting is one of the things that makes us a great civilization. Most people have trouble believing that cockfighting goes on in a place like Connecticut. Most people assume that the only way we could have cockfighting here would be if the chickens wore little Ralph Lauren shirts and tried to ram each other in little BMWs.

Au contraire. Recently, eleven men were arrested in the Connecticut town of Shelton in a cockfighting raid. The news accounts said it was "the biggest cockfighting arrest in Shelton history." So don't get tripped up if you are in a sports bar and someone asks you a trivia question about the top three Shelton cockfighting busts, because this baby rewrote the record books.

I think the arrested parties used the old defense of claiming they happened upon two chickens hooked up in a donnybrook and were just trying to break it up.

Still, that is hardly the subject of this book. No, this book is about Life, and what can be done about it.

You don't hear a lot of talk about Life, as a commodity, except from insurance agents, graduation speakers and self-help books.

These sources are at pains to tell us what Life is (a

bowl of cherries; for the living; what you make of it; spreading out before you like a vast indecipherable tundra) or is not (a bowl of cherries; a free ride; for the squeamish).

We have been told these things, and where has it gotten us? Mainly, it has put me off cherries.

It is worrisome to suppose that Life is what we make of it. Life is one of quite a few things that should come assembled but don't. What if we already know that we are not gifted at making one thing out of another? Where does that leave us? Can we take Life back and get the floor model?

These are all good questions, and it is best not to think about any of them. Better to just put Life as far from your thoughts as possible, to think about Life seldom if at all (although, invariably, having made that decision, you will pass by the water cooler at work one day and hear it said of you—your name being Farkins—"They say Farkins is hanging on for dear Life").

Once you get going on Life, Time is bound to come up. Time marches on or, if it dares, flies (unless it is running out). Time waits for no man and is of the essence. Just as discussions of Life tend to signify a general lack of liveliness, no one has so much Time on his hands as the person who feels compelled to talk about It. Some good advice about Time: it is generally better to make it than to do it. As it turns out, most of adult Life is lived out, unnervingly, in the interim.

If this book were a graduation speech, we would also have to get into The World. Fortunately, we may be able to dodge around it. (Graduates are often informed that they are now ready to go out into The World, which makes them wonder where they have been heretofore.

Graduates are urged to make The World a better place. So what is The World? A fixer-upper? A handyman's special? What is Life—see above—a scratch and dent sale?)

This book will not resemble any other self-help book you have read. For one thing, I would assume that the other ones have, at their hearts, at least some slight nugget of genuine hope that you can improve your life, whereas I am strictly interested in getting enough capital to clear up the above-mentioned jai alai situation.

In the pages ahead, I'll be introducing some actual case histories which I have conscientiously fabricated, based on news items I read while waiting in the supermarket checkout lines. Also, you will find some of the famous Lost Ann Landers Letters. These, of course, are the letters recovered from an earthenware jar at the site of the Tigris and Euphrates civilization, although they are thought to be from the period right after Tigris and Euphrates retired and sold all the fixtures, goodwill, etc., to a big Hittite outfit.

(Perhaps you have heard the theory that the Lost Ann Landers Letters were brought to earth, centuries ago, by a race of superior beings from a distant planet in order that they might serve as archetypes for all future letters to newspaper advice columnists—a popular notion among elements of the lunatic fringe, which is the key target market for my work.)

Finally, I must apologize for one other feature of this book. In order to roll back some of the huge deficits created by my first book, Doubleday asked if I would be willing to put a few classified advertisements in this book. I went along with it. Maybe this places me even farther outside the groves of literature than ever. It's not the kind of thing Baudelaire would have done.

So, are you ready to start reading this book? Good. Put on some loose-fitting clothing and, whatever you do, don't stare directly into it.

L O S E

WEIGHT

→ **THROUGH**

GREAT SEX

★★★★ **WITH**

CELEBRITIES!

(the Elvis way)

1

Once More into the Britch:
The Whole Man and Woman Thing

I read a book called *How to Find a Husband in 30 Days.*

Not that I was in the market for one. I already have a wife, so it seems kind of greedy to start thinking about adding on a husband. Where would he sleep? Not in my bed, that's for sure. It's already too crowded, what with this wife I was mentioning, plus a couple of dogs, a gopher and the Lithuanian viceroy.

It would be nice to have a husband around to hammer and saw things and put the storm windows up, but you know husbands: one week of that and they start asking to be put through law school.

No, I read this book out of sheer nosiness, much the same way I read personal ads.

Which brings up an interesting point. Married people are great readers of personal ads. I suppose it's like a dieter watching people eat exotic things. Also, because of the anonymity, people seem to describe their wants and needs more honestly than they might if you met them, say, at a tax audit.

As time begins to pass me by at a brisker clip, I find myself reading about wants and needs I wasn't even aware of. Stuff like:

QBO: Seeks MZH, left-handed, vivacious, familiar with writings of Nasir-Fong and willing to try same, esp. Krummelman manuever, must bring own eggbeater, llama. No strings. Well, *some* strings. Send daguerreotype, artist's rendering. No Iowans, no mesomorphs. Send strings.

Most of the ads are not so interesting. The bulk of them make you want nothing so much as a few shares of stock in a candle factory. "Enjoy candlelight dinners, long walks on the beach," they say. There appear to be so many of these people that it's a wonder they haven't worn away our Continental Shelf what with their dogged tramping up and down our nation's beaches, sifting sand through their wax-coated fingers.

Not everyone who writes a personal ad is so certain about his or her wants and needs. I once read an ad from a woman who said she "may want to be swept off her feet."

She doesn't know? I suppose that's legitimate. Maybe even a motion sickness issue there. Getting swept off your feet is not the kind of deal where you can take a Dramamine an hour ahead of time.

Still, it's interesting to see someone trying to work out her feelings on this subject right before our very prying eyes. I suppose someday I'll read: "Attractive married couple seeks third party for . . . that is, we sense that we're moving toward . . . No, no, this can't be right. But we can't help what we feel . . . Maybe we're not ready. Look, let's just forget the whole thing. Unless you're interested. And strongly resemble Estes Kefauver. Gender not important. Box 23, Passaic."

For some people, knowing what they don't want is the important thing. You see ads that go on and on: "No fats, no fems, no studmuffins, no dweebs, no ginks, no low-ballers, no high-toned women, no midnight ramblers, no, no, Nanette. No! Nobody. Go 'way. Box 1074."

The ads in *The New York Review of Books* are fun because people drag in literature. One advertiser said she likes "Carver's poems." I wracked my brain. George Washington Carver was a pretty all-around guy, but did he write poems?

> *I think that I shall never see nuts*
> *As multifarious as peanuts.*

Another advertiser claimed to like "Tolstoi, Austin, Raymond Chandler." Austin? If it were Jane Austen, she'd know how to spell it. (If it were, and she didn't, would you tell her on the first date?) Maybe it's Austin, Texas. Or Alfred Austin, who wrote

> *But the sweetest smile she ever wore*
> *Was the smile she wore in death.*

Dear me. Let's hope that's not what she means.

Actually, a lot of great poetry resembles personal ads. Whitman probably wrote the longest one. "I celebrate myself and sing myself, etc." There's a lot of that in personal ads.

Pretty much everybody is, at the very least, "attractive and vivacious." It's almost a civil right—right up there with fair housing, education and cable television—that every American is allowed to claim comeliness in personal ads. You kind of have to adjust the whole scale. By the standards of personal ad bravura, just merely "attractive and vivacious" is so rock-bottom, we're probably talking Quasimodo here.

Some of the ads go to peculiar lengths of self-celebration. "You'll enjoy one date with me more than one month with Joe Namath," one guy wrote.

What?

That degree of smugness is, I think, an eighties phenomenon, a by-product of the Reagan-inspired lack of reasonable doubt about ourselves. I kept looking for that ultimate ad that would read:

> SWM. Single, attractive, professional, affluent man enjoys long walks on beach, fireside chats, Proust, Truffaut, tennis, skiing, sailing, travel, etc. Nonsmoker. Own Porsche. Sense of humor. Communicative. Sensitive. Firm but giving. Self-sufficient. Not into games. Did mention Porsche? Good. Not looking for companion, lover, etc. Basically happy by self. Just thought you'd like to know.

Maybe in the nineties, we'll swing back to thirsting, questing, reaching out for one another in the darkness. Like Whitman:

> *Failing to fetch me at first keep encouraged,*
> *Missing me in one place search another,*
> *I stop somewhere waiting for you.*

Either that or simply writing and reading these advertisements will take the place of actually venturing out and meeting the people behind them. Each ad that you read is a little bit like a brief affair, except that the person does not ever call you up, years later, at 3 A.M., drunk and sobbing.

Once you start thinking about these things, time slips away, which is why it's probably a good idea to allow a little more than thirty days to find a mate. My advice is to do it like baseball: start in earnest around April. If you're still mired in a slump by the All-Star break, you better shake up your lineup, bring up some hot young phenom from Pawtucket.

These doubts notwithstanding, I plunged into *How to Find a Husband in 30 Days* by Wendy Stehling. It is important to understand that Stehling's previous contribution to world literature was called *Thin Thighs in 30 Days.* So this second book is Stehling's way of helping all those women out there shambling around on pencil-thin thighs. They want to land a hunk of beef before their legs give out.

Stehling's book suffers from the two major misconceptions of the genre.

1. The notion that what men need, in the way of flattery, is nothing less than a female Uriah Heep.
2. The notion that what men want, in the bedroom, is nothing less than a carnal strategist who plans her every move with the precision of a female Earl Weaver (which is necessary, in this author's view, only if the woman in any way resembles Earl Weaver).

Anyway, some of the subterfuges Stehling suggests include:

- *Talk about cars.* Stehling imagines that we men are suckers for car talk. She encourages women to bone up on it. Speaking for those guys among us who could distinguish a spark plug from a pomegrante only with great difficulty and a certain amount of luck, I say it might be deflating to have a woman lean over toward me in a cozy restaurant booth and murmur: "I just put a 442 Hamaker-Flusskrebs engine in a '73 GTO with polyglas spoilers and a 5.1 cambered alluvial retro-valve with headers, plus I got that sucker jacked three inches above the max with custom mags and a coaxial fiber-pinion differential that . . ."

- *Smile at your date.* Stehling boasts of returning from one date with a face (her own) that ached from smiling. Somehow, it sounds like a long evening on both ends. No one is saying you should go the Tom Landry route here, but certainly if your date announces, "I think I just ran over a bunny rabbit," you could let your corners droop a little.

- *Wear erotic underwear.* Stehling is very big on wild underthings and even takes the position that "all woman look good in garter belts." Probably the best thing to do here is to pause while each reader summons to mind a favorite example or two of why this is simply not so. It is true, however, that a garter belt or something of that ilk can take a woman who is . . . and . . . Ah, never mind. I've found that this whole subject is a great way to get into unpleasant arguments with women. Anyway, you can go too far with this underwear stuff. Something black and a little lacy is just great. Something with a battery-powered windmill blade is probably overreaching.

- *While you are talking about the federal deficit, cross your legs a few times . . ."* No kidding. This is in the book. What does it mean? If a lot of women did it, would the dollar stay bullish?

- *Get rid of the clutter in your house before inviting a man over.* This is good advice. I had a blind date many years ago with a woman whose apartment looked like what the Manson Family would consider a "fixer-upper." It appeared to be inhabited by about eighteen members of an anti-dishwashing (or even -dishscraping) cult, although all I could see on the premises was her and a dog. The dog was involved in some kind of custody situation, which the woman began to explain to me before breaking out (quite justifiably, I thought) right before my eyes in hives.

  So, anyway, get rid of the clutter. (Not that massive housecleaning would have brought this particular blind date back from *Omen VI* territory.)

  To drive home her point about clutter, Stehling —unable to execute a prose equivalent of crossing and uncrossing her legs—urges her 30-Day Wonders, "Don't have a dozen candles around the bed." Well . . .

  Depends on whom you're having over. The Pope might be put rather at ease.

- *Have a sense of humor.* Stehling, it turns out, does not have in mind Dorothy Parker and epigrams flying around the Algonquin Round Table. She mentions a man who likes the way his girlfriend pinches his behind, even in public places. (The communion rail?)

  I suppose pinching is all right, in its place. It shouldn't expand into hand buzzers and rubber chickens, unless you and your guy are a couple of aging vaudevillians.

- *Cultivate a taste in music.* This is good advice, as far as it goes. I have noticed that single women's personal disillusionments sometimes show up in the forms of massive collections of disgruntled blues records by Billie Holiday, with the occasional frisson of white bourgeois angst tossed in (usually in the form of a few Laura Nyro platters). There is nothing wrong with this when you're alone or shooting the bull with the gals, but don't let it spill over into your dates. It's flat-out counterproductive to pour the wine, dim the lights—Stehling, by the by, says the lights should be pink, presumably to remind the man of the one place he ever felt safe with a woman, the womb—and then turning on a tinny recording of Bessie Smith singing "That Man Done Did What He Said He Hadn't Ought to of Done an' Shot My Cat an' Took My Money Besides."

• *Say his name a lot. And be knowledgeable about his job. And don't drink beer. And blow in his ear. And wear skirts. And fuzzy sweaters.*

All this? Just for a lousy man?

"Well, Buford Pennypacker, you are just about the best polythene extruder I ever pssssssss did see. I like the way you, Buford Pennypacker, psssss use the T67 broach-clamp on the left stanchion extrusion psssssssss. No beer, thanks, Buford Pennypacker. Did some fuzz go up your nose? Sorry about that, Buford Pennypa . . ."

You know, there may be some merit in punting the whole deal and raising llamas on a unisex communal farm.

2

Case History: The Man Who Mistook Himself for Michael Jackson's Love Child

Donald H., a carpenter from Mottled Cape, Michigan, read about the $150 million paternity suit filed against Michael Jackson and became concerned that he, too, might be Michael Jackson's love child. Recent studies indicate that between 8 and 14 percent of all Americans share this concern about themselves.

Here are Donald's words.

I am having a heck of a time getting my parents to talk to me about it.

I have assured them that, no matter what comes out, I will always consider them to be my parents. I mean, after all these years of neglect, Michael Jackson is not going to get away with just showing up on my doorstep as though nothing had happened.

Did Michael Jackson coach my Little League team? Did Michael Jackson take me out to the International House of Pancakes for a stack of Extra Nutties with Boysenberry Drambuie Syrup after Sunday church? Did Michael Jackson show me how to use the rope swing down at the old swimmin' hole?

No.

My own parents never did any of these things either, but that's hardly the point, is it? If I am Michael Jackson's love child, he should have been there for me.

Where was he when I skinned my knee learning to ride my bike? Probably showing Bubbles, that stupid chimpanzee of his, the new electric train set. I bet Bubbles had a better bike than I did.

You bet I'm bitter.

Still, my parents are very reluctant to talk about this. Whatever happened, they say, let it sleep in the past.

But I have had a few clues.

For instance, I can moonwalk. I never had to think about it. I could just do it. I have to wonder where I get this from. Last Thanksgiving, after the meal, I coyly suggested that our whole family do a little moonwalking, just to help our dinners settle. I showed them some moves and, get this, nobody could do it. Not Mom, Dad, my sister GiGi, Uncle Jim, nobody. Grandma said her brother Montpelier had, for a few years, done something similar, but everybody thought this was because he had taken a lick in the head from a sling barometer.

Then there was my eighth birthday. Right in the middle of the party, the doorbell rang, and it was a guy delivering two llamas and the deed to fourteen blocks of prime Detroit commercial real estate. From "a friend."

"Probably the Pedells," said my mother, laughing a nervous titter.

Well, Jeff and Drew Pedell had been real good friends of mine and had moved out of the neighborhood a couple of years beforehand. I am sure they would have bought me a nice gift, but there was something about the faraway look in my dad's eyes.

At my high school graduation, as I went up to get my diploma, I happened to look toward the back row of the audience and saw a guy in an admiral's uniform and Central American dictator sunglasses getting up to leave. Afterward, I went to check his seat. I found a surgical mask lying there.

It's the not knowing that eats away at me. I try to talk to my parents about this, but they just shrug and say, "You never went hungry . . ."

And there's no arguing about that. Whenever it came down to a choice between paying for the braces I needed on my teeth or buying themselves the skeleton of a famous sufferer of an obscure disease, my parents always put my needs first and did without.

Now that I'm grown-up and doing well on my own, I've actually been tucking a little money aside each week so that someday I can surprise them with that skeleton they've dreamed of.

I hate myself for this, but I can't help wondering what I may have missed by not growing up in Michael's house. Probably he would have bought me a little bitty child-sized hyperbaric oxygen chamber so we could lie around together on Sunday mornings while one of the androids read the funny papers to us. And Liz Taylor as my godmother? Boy . . .

So sue me. I yearn to be tucked in at night by the fatherly touch of a gloved hand; to drift off to sleep surrounded by beaming mannequins and a friendly python; to hear, in the last moments before warm, dark slumber claims me, the soft voice of my real father crooning, "Wanna Be Startin' Somethin'?"

3

Lost Ann Landers Letter Number One

DEAR ANN LANDERS: A few years ago, you published an inspirational poem, and it touched me so that I clipped it out and carried it around in my wallet until it became all wore out and frayed and yellow, and eventually I picked up some kinda infection from it so that nobody would shake hands with me for about four and a half years, not to mention the smell. Boy, it was a good poem though. Anyway, recently my wallet fell into a nuclear breeder reactor, but I fished it out so as not to lose the poem, but it was pretty much illegible by then and some of the *e*'s had a tendency to leap off the page and scurry around the room, and anyway, "Dan" (my second marriage, his first) says we can't afford reading glasses for me, even though I notice nothing is too good for those exotic pigeons (their third marriage) he keeps on the roof. Anyway, I took the clipping of the poem to this research lab in Dubuque where they have been analyzing the Shroud of Murray, an ancient fabric which, it is believed, St. Peter was planning to use for new slipcovers. Even the institute scientists' (their first marriage) most advanced carbon treatments, however, were not able to bring out the poem and the only word they were able to reconsruct was "earwax," which I don't remember from the first time around. Any chance you could reprint the poem? Boy, I have half a mind to go up there with some Ginsu cutlery and turn those pigeons into moussaka. What do you think the deal is with "Dan" and those pigeons anyway? And what kind of jerk goes around with quotation marks hanging over his name? I am,

—POOPED IN PADUCAH

4

Cher and Shere Alike

Shortly after the publication of her book *Men and Love,* human relations researcher Shere Hite tangled with a West Haven, Connecticut, limousine driver who informed her he was under orders not to drive her from New York to New Haven because she was ninety minutes late.

The man said Hite punched him in the nose after he called her "dear."

The incident inspired us to conduct the study which comprises this chapter. It was one of the most massive surveys of human behavior ever conducted. We left more than 640 questionnaires in pro wrestling arenas, bowling alleys, coffeeshops catering to the human research trade and sparring gyms.

It is dangerous to generalize. Still, we feel safe in saying that the American woman of today—except for you and you and you there in the back—wants nothing so much as to haul off and pop somebody in the beezer.

With that in mind, we present the findings of "The Hit Report: Why Women Clobber."

- *Only 44 percent of the women said they derived full satisfaction from punching their husbands or mates in the nose.*

  "In the beginning of our relationship, punching Zelmo in the nose was great. He had tremendous footwork and could backpedal for hours. He used a lot of head fakes, and I would only be able to graze him with my jab. As the years passed, however, he started dropping his left quite a bit, and I was able to get to him much quicker. Nowadays it's pretty much wham, bam, thank-you-ma'am. I set him up with a simple combination, and boom, I turn out his lights. He doesn't seem to understand that the preparation is important to me."

  "Cadmus is a premature knockout. If I so much as tap him, he's down on the canvas for a mandatory eight count. I've begged him to do some road work, skip some rope, but no go."

- *78 percent of the women said they had, at one time or another, gone outside the marriage to punch someone in the nose.*

  "Sometimes I feel dirty afterward, but I'm hooked on the excitement. Last month, it was the eighteen-year-old who delivers the groceries. He was coming up the stairs, and I thought: I can take him. *Pow.* He folds up like a ladder. There's celery rolling into the corner, a can of Dinty Moore bouncing down the stairs, Slim Jims all over the place. I tried having my husband hold a full grocery bag, but it wasn't the same."

- *24 percent said they had experimented with wrestling.*

  "Gerald came home from work, and I was there at the door in my Greco-Roman outfit. *Zing.* I go for the takedown, and I get him in a chicken wing, set up for the pin. He tries to scissor out, but I'm expecting that, so I use the opening to move to the full nelson. He tries to work his way across to the foyer, but the ref warns him for stalling. I move in for the crab ride; he tries to sit out; I get him in the cradle. *Bam.* I pin him. The earth moved."

- *60 percent complained that men seemed detached.*

"I make an effort. I get out my flimsiest Everlast trunks, put the Howard Cosell *Bolero* record on the stereo, read a little Hemingway to him. He goes through the motions, but I can tell he'd rather be out palling around with his trainer, his cut man and the rest of his entourage."

- *95 percent said that the size of a man's nose is unimportant to them.*

"On the other hand, I wouldn't kick Cyrano de Bergerac out of the ring, if you know what I mean."

- *65 percent of the women said the emotional side of punching someone in the nose is as important as the physical. Men, they say, do not understand this.*

"I've punched people in the nose on some nights when I've really felt *on.* My breathing is great, my rhythm is there, my concentration is perfect. But if the emotion isn't right, if I don't feel genuinely inconvenienced and condescended to, it's actually a pretty hollow feeling. I might as well be working out on a bag."

- *56 percent of the women said punching people in the nose is less important to them now.*

"I think the Pugilistic Revolution kind of overemphasized the importance of it. Frankly, I'd be just as happy staying home with a glass of wine and a nice questionnaire."

5

Case History: The Man Who Thought He Was Married to Joan Collins

Ward, thirty-three, is a liposuction technician in Bursting-at-the-Seams, Delaware. At the time of the Joan Collins–Peter Holm divorce trial, he was one of several hundred men to come forward with the same astonishing claim. It is difficult to ascertain how many, if any, of these men were actually married to Joan Collins, but the Bureau of Weights and Measures has agreed to consider funding a major archival research project into this matter, with a projected budget of $4.5 million (that figure representing a staff of three people working for about three weeks, and then throwing the standard $3.8 million office party occasioned by the completion of any federal project).

In the meanwhile, the reader must judge Ward's story on its own merits.

My heart goes out to Peter Holm, because I know how tight Joan can be with a dollar once she has tossed you aside like a box of imported chocolates, each one bitten into in the vain quest for perfection.

I met Joan Collins several years ago, shortly after the disbanding of my rock group Full Neurological Work-up. I was eating alone at Chuck E. Cheese, the then-trendy video pizza franchise, when a large, burly man approached my table and said, "Joan Collins would like to marry you. Come this way."

I was not allowed to finish my pineapple and ham pizza, which cost $4.65.

The man brought me to a secluded airstrip where I boarded Joan Collins's jet. The pilot had been married to Joan the day before, on the other side of the International Date Line, and had been divorced by her that morning in Los Angeles, but he was concerned that he might still be married to her in certain parts of the world where it was still yesterday.

He asked if I had any change so he could call Djakarta and see if he was, by any chance, still married there. I loaned him $2.85, mostly quarters. I never saw any of that again.

I arrived at Joan's house in Beverly Hills, and she and I talked for a few minutes, during which time we fell deeply in love. That night, I escorted her to a party at the Playboy Mansion, but the Playboy Mansion was full to capacity, so we went to a second party at the Crossword Puzzle Digest Mansion, and from there to the Rodale's Organic Gardening Mansion, where we danced until 2 A.M. to a band consisting entirely of rototillers tuned to different—although not all that different—pitches and fell, if possible, more deeply in love than ever.

We saddled up two burros and rode into the desert. We lay on a mesa, our nostrils gorged with the scents of jasmine and sandalwood. A blinding ruby light filled our minds, and our spirit animals appeared to us and urged us to wed. We rode back and were married at dawn in the Radio-Controlled Car Hobbyist Journal Mansion, by the publisher of that fine magazine.

During our marriage, which lasted for two days and well into the afternoon of a third, I realized that Joan was deeply in need of someone to manage her financial affairs, and I tried to serve in that capacity.

I reviewed her portfolio and explained to her, for example, that her previous financial advisers had served her poorly by urging an investment in a mine operated by the Seven Dwarves, inasmuch as they were fictional characters. I got her a check-cashing card at the supermarket and explained about double coupons.

Joan's electric bills were high, and I gave her quite a few tips on how to keep them down, especially by dusting light bulbs. This was on the second day of our marriage, around 3:00 or 3:15 P.M.—a time of, perhaps, our greatest happiness together, as I look back now.

We were in such bliss that I never could have imagined things going sour as fast as they did. By the morning of the third day, though, some of our closest friends had begun to sense that we were just not the same two people we had been. In the afternoon, Joan opened up on me with semiautomatic weapon fire and screamed, "Get out. Get out." It was impossible for me to deny the reality any longer. Our marriage, I sensed, was in trouble.

I begged her to consider counseling, but it seemed as if we were speaking two different languages. For one thing, she thought I meant some kind of marksmanship instruction.

I'm sure you read of the divorce. Since then, Joan has spurned all contact with me. I have suffered tremendous hardship. During our marriage, I became accustomed to a certain lifestyle. I wear $3,500 sports jackets made of dried Panamanian mushrooms and $800 shoes made of live armadillos. My haircut alone requires that a team of specialists from the Follicle Institute of Geneva be flown in at considerable expense, plus these guys usually want a little walking-around money while they're in town.

Joan will not help me out with any of this. Worse still, I figure I am out some $68.45 for the pizza, the phone call, a round of drinks I bought, some gummed labels, a Garden Weasel, what have you.

I have since married a wonderful girl who knows about Joan and accepts me anyway. We are very happy together. But when you have lived the kind of life I had with Joan—a life most of you know only from watching Robin Leach—you are never, ever, the same person you were before.

Don't let anyone tell you different.

6

How to Marry a Fanatic (and Other Alternatives to Single Life)

I believe in turning negatives into positives, so when I read a few years ago that a single woman over forty stood a better chance of being killed by a terrorist than of finding a husband, I asked myself: How can these two troubled and problematic groups work *for* each other?

The answer was pretty darned obvious. Women of forty should just up and marry terrorists.

Stop and consider. Your basic terrorist is young, lonely, driven by impulses he scarcely understands. What he needs is a stable relationship with a woman who's been around the kiosk a couple of times. Give these guys a week or two of regular, well-balanced meals, bedtime at a reasonable hour, a William Hurt movie on the weekend. You'll marvel at the changes.

For the women, it's a chance to find a man with a demonstrated belief in commitment—a man who's not a wimp, a man who's interested in something more substantial than just a quick fling.

There are, however a few key concerns to be factored in:

- Many terrorists do not feel comfortable in singles' bars. But more and more clubs are offering special events such as "Jihad Hours," "Jackal Night" and the ever-popular "Conga Line of Death." A woman interested in meeting a fanatic should attend these and be prepared to field such come-ons as "So, what satanic, sniveling, rapacious Western sign are you?" or "Do you debase yourself on these premises often, Western prostitute?"
- A cleverly worded personal ad, placed in a publication such as *Better Holes and Carbines,* may lure a shy terrorist out of hiding. To wit:

SWF, 40-ish, vivacious, tired of the bazaar scene, enjoys good books, long walks on burning sand, candlelight chanting, nasal ablutions. Seeks younger man for veiled thrills, wild-eyed dedication.

- A woman who winds up dating a terrorist should be prepared to assert herself. Many terrorists were mama's boys. They are accustomed to getting their ways and will often expect their dates to wait around while they and their friends plot the overthrow of capitalism long into the night.

  You will have to let Achmed or Ian or Carlos know that *you* have a limited amount of recreational time and that a three-hour discussion of makeshift grenade launchers is not your idea of a sparkling night. (See my book *Men Who Hate Civilization (and the Women Who Hijack Them.)*
- Let's say you get through all the awkward stages and

decide you were meant for each other. The wedding itself may be the biggest hurdle you ever face.

Do the planning yourself. The rap against terrorist weddings is there's never enough food, the band stinks (sometimes literally) and there's always some loopy out-of-town guest who fires his Uzi into the cake before it's cut (chew carefully).

Just picking out a china pattern with a terrorist can be an ordeal.

Jennifer G., thirty-two, a Manhattan interior designer and Morris dancer, recalls: "He said, 'Each plate must be showing a wondrous tableau from the Ayatollah's life, such as the flogging of a godless imperialist harlot, plus picture of the despot Reagan whose jaws are to be seen dripping with the blood of Allah's innocent people.' We settled on Royal Doulton, but I had to give in on towels. He insisted on sackcloth."

- If you marry a Libyan, keep your own name. That's the advice of Cleveland account executive and tumbler Mimi Qenoze, née Plotzwinkle, who suffered through the inconsistencies of modern transliteration. "The wedding announcement in the *Tribune* said Qujoutz and the *Plain Dealer* spelled it Ghamos. My checks read Kueqosca; the IRS does it Quatzna; and the yard guys call me Mrs. Kenosha."

The big question, though, seems to be: Is it worth it? Do they ever settle down?

You'll know the answer the first time the phone rings for him and it's:

"Anok, sacred comrade, today we strike fear into the engorged, dung-eating tick of Western imperialism."

"I cannot, my trusted friend. Things pile up. Today I am lashing the Scourge of Heaven against the unholy crabgrass, driving the devils of mildew from our exalted rec room and placing the righteous shoulder of belief to the removal of storm windows."

Then you will have found the husband inside your terrorist.

7

A Special Announcement

As an exclusive service to readers of this book, we are reporting the following weather cancellations. These groups will not meet tonight due to the bad weather. Stay home and continue reading this book.

This service is not being offered to people reading books by Tom Clancy, Judith Krantz or Immanuel Kant.

- The Episcopalian Primal Scream meeting at St. Franz's Church is canceled. People who felt they had an especially good scream ready this week may tape it and present it next week, although they will also be required to produce an original, live scream at that time.
- The Irritability Support Group meeting at Jim's Corners is canceled. Okay? Are you satisfied? We were going to postpone it but . . . we just didn't, all right? Look, you think you can run this group better, Mr. Big Shot, just go ahead. It's all yours. We

wash our hands. Well? Okay, then, don't second-guess us.

Jerk.

- The Little Bitty Eeeny Weeny Fuzzy Wuzzy Willy Winkum Dirty Ducky Diaper Tweedle-de-deedle-de-arra-sh'boom-blam!-blam!-aiieeeee Day Care Center in Blystred Oakes will close its itsy-bitsy doors early today, when the ducky-wucky's big toe is on the twelve and the ducky-wucky's little wing is on the one. All the daddies and mommies should come and pick up their little pixies right after Mr. Milk and Mrs. Cracker Time, except for the mommy and daddy of Joey, who busted out of maximum security this morning. He is now at-large and is believed to have Mrs. Fairfellow with him as a hostage. (Mr. Bibblegrooks was on the table for three hours, the doctors believe they got most of the Lego.)
- Greater Widgefield Belch-Enders is postponed until Tuesday. Urp! Excuse me.
- Classes at Wamogo Regional High School will not be affected in any way. It's just that Wamogo is such a funny name, we like to mention it.
- Tonight's Etruscan Goat Dancing at the Cheshire Community Center is canceled. However, persons who do not bring their own goats to dance with and had asked that one be provided for them should go to the center and pick theirs up and dance with it just a little, inasmuch as its expectations will have been built up. Mrs. Upsala will be there waiting with the goats until eight, and then she doesn't know what she'll do.
- The Radio-Controlled Airplane Hobbyist Club of Perno will meet as scheduled. However, people in-

volved in this sort of activity are, it should be observed, geeks.

- The First Holy Sepulcher-in-the-Seed Turtle-Handling Church of the Divine in Derby announces that, due to the Promised Storm signaling the End of the Last Days of the Factory Close-out Sale of This World and the Judgment Upon the Wicked and the Spinning of Their Unrighteous Chainless and Unstudded Tires in the Ruts of Their Own Devising and the Fishtailing of the Sinners Doomed to Skid into the Ditch of Perdition, there will be no potluck supper tonight.
- Wamogo wamogo wamogo.
- The Rap Session for the Chronically Indecisive is flat-out canceled, and that's that. Unless you think it might let up. We heard one guy in the luncheonette say it might, but I don't know if he'd heard a weather report or if he was just . . . Gee, hate to miss a meeting if it's not that bad out. If we postponed it a couple of hours, you figure the plows . . . What are other groups doing?

8

Paper Cow

I have a new book about how to organize the paper in your life, or at least I did have it. It's gone now. Lost under all this paper. I believe it might have merged its atoms with those of the Funny Instructions pile, where it was seen loitering not hours before its disappearance.

The Funny Instructions pile consists mostly of badly translated and therefore incomprehensible instructions on how to use various foreign-made products. Anyway, the Funny Instructions pile itself has drifted out of sight in the general tectonic grinding of the surface of my desk, so it's all kind of a moot issue.

Unfortunately, the Moot Issues pile caught fire a couple of days ago and crews have not yet brought the blaze under control.

Even if the Funny Instructions pile should never be seen again, it is gratifying to know that I have made several backup copies of its crown jewel and filed them in various other locales.

The jewel in question is the "Guide for Setting-Up

Iglu," a document I have saved for three or four years now, a document which has become my own personal Koran and *Rubáiyát,* scrolled into one.

The "Guide for Setting-Up Iglu" involves some kind of tent, which was bought by someone I know in New Zealand. It contains such instructions as "Now you can beat those herrings (2) through the metalrings inside earth."

In our moments of uncertainty, the Guide reassures us: "Reperatursets are obtainable at any specialty shops."

Most importantly, it states: "You have in your mind that the tent can burn. So comping it under the observation of safety. Please obey the laws of healthy human understanding."

But what are they? Over the years, I have come to think of my life as nothing so much as a quest for the laws of healthy human understanding.

Anyway, there is little chance of my losing the Guide because I have followed my own Rule 7A of paperwork management: "Make loads of copies of anything even remotely important."

I don't know what the rest of my rules are, because (not being terribly important) they're lost. I *can,* however, put my hands right on a well-aged press clipping from London about a woman who had a one-and-a-quarter-inch nail stuck up her nose for thirty years and didn't know it. "I must have got it stuck there when I was a toddler. It's incredible" is the quote of the woman, whose name—wonderfully enough—is Wendy Clamp.

I can also find a very old memo from someone (it's unsigned) listing the names of persons involved in the Society for the Restoration and Preservation of Red M&Ms, but—since I think the red ones were restored not long ago—maybe this should go to Moot Issues once the fire dies down.

And (we're definitely in the bonus situation here) I can also find a correction notice from a Connecticut newspaper explaining that a recent advertisement for Amazing Stores contained a photograph of George Bush where a picture of "Mr. Amazing" was supposed to have appeared.

Ah, me.

I challenge the woman who wrote the missing book on paperwork organizing—Hemphill, I believe, was her name—to find anything on her desk that is one half so spiritually bracing and life-enhancing as what I have mentioned.

I would like to mention my overriding principle of paper management—the Principle of Askance-ness. That is, you will never find any particular thing if you are looking for it very specifically. You have to fool your mind into thinking it is looking for something else or, better yet, for nothing at all. Just kind of mussing about.

This is no easy feat and has taken me years of study in the Far East to achieve.

Let us say you are looking for a pamphlet on perspiration. You will never find it unless you convince your mind you are looking for, say, a news clipping about the last cow on Gibraltar. And there's the danger that, should you find the pamphlet, you will no longer remember you want it and go on looking for the cow thing.

This is not so far-fetched. I own a year-old clipping about the Gibraltar cow (who was leaving at the time) and am looking around for it. People out in the world take great pains to make sure I am well-informed about cows. When the whole business about cow flatulence contributing to the Greenhouse Effect came to light recently, five or six people troubled themselves to send me clippings on the subject.

The pamphlet on perspiration I have right here. I don't want it, and I don't know how I got it. If you lost it and want it back, give me a call. But remember to ask for the cow thing instead, or I'll never find it.

9

What to Do When Your Spouse Is Away

This might not seem to you like a very critical life issue if you are not married or if you have been married a long, long time or if you are not sure whether or not you are married or if you are just lying in a Sumerian tomb waiting for someone to reanimate you so that you may visit destruction upon the infidels of this generation.

But take my word for it, you don't really know very much about your own life until your spouse goes away for a few days.

The worst thing about it is the way people—people who should know better—leer at you and say, "Hubba-hubba" upon hearing that your spouse is away. This is a natural human motor reflex and has nothing to do with the moral uprightness of the hubba-hubbee. When the Archbishop of Canterbury's wife is away, people say to him "Hubba-hubba" or whatever passes for "Hubba-hubba" down Canterbury way.

The latent assumption is that the Archbishop will observe a decent interval of about five minutes before racing down to Main Street to wait for Marilyn Monroe to stand over a subway grate. The reality is that the Archbishop peers around his house as though it were a strange new place, as though he had been abandoned there by a UFO, with sketchy instructions on how to care for Liberace's brain.

Far from having any opportunity to watch Marilyn's farthingales invert, the Archbishop is suddenly, sinkingly aware that he has no idea where his mitres are kept. He is pretty sure he has to consecrate somebody or something in about an hour, but he has no idea who or what or where. Out the window, he can see his dog Andrew running toward the woods with his crozier in its mouth.

I am not—as this book goes to press, anyway—the Archbishop of Canterbury, but I have been through my own secular version of those travails.

"I can handle this," I told the dog confidently the last time my wife shipped off to some family wedding I had wangled my craven self out of.

The dog looked at me with grave misgivings. The dog suspects I am not a detail person. Good for throwing balls and sticks, yes, but not for the little particulars of which households are constituted.

A man's home is his Disneyland, in the sense that there is a good deal going on behind the scenes, by way of maintenance, that he cannot even guess at as he drifts through the main attractions.

Almost immediately after my wife's departure, there was a fine layer of sand in the bed. I brushed it out. It was still there. I shook it out. It didn't budge. Ah, what the heck, I thought (which, I later discovered, is exactly what they kept saying in Amityville).

A day or so passed. My wife called from Chicago. Our towels, it seemed, had been preying on her mind.

"They're probably damp. You should wash them. They might be getting mildewed. Check them, and if they . . ."

Now, gee, I hate to reinforce gender stereotypes, but in all the ages since Odysseus set forth on the wine-dark sea, has any man, a few days into a journey, started wondering about the towels back home?

"Towels?" I thundered into the phone. "You're calling me to talk about towels?"

"Well, if they're not too damp . . . What's the weather been like?"

"Believe me, I'm on top of this. I've got the aneroid barometer out, and I'm watching the developments with great care. I think it's fair to say an air of measured caution hangs over the whole situation. It's touch and go with the towels. If something takes a sudden turn, I'm prepared to move and move fast."

That seemed to satisfy her.

I hung up the phone and asked the dog, "Do you remember seeing any towels?"

I went upstairs and lay down in the sand to ponder my next move. The truth is, the last time I used a washing machine, the Seabees had to be called in.

Time, for a married man on his own, loses its contours. He sleeps when he is tired, eats when he is hungry, shaves when he is grizzled, bathes when the neighbors complain. Life takes on a gauzy, hallucinatory quality.

The dog, sensing a leadership vacuum, made a power grab. He set up a junta, began eating off my plate, affected sunglasses, epaulets and a military braid.

Some grackles built a nest in the bed, near the mound of gravel forming in the southwest corner.

The phone rang. I found it in the piano. I was wearing a hussar's uniform, a shako and flippers. I couldn't remember why. One of my basketball sneakers was in the blender. A lavender towel slithered around a corner, reared up and hissed at me.

"Who is this?" I shouted into the basketball sneaker.

"Hello?" said my wife's voice from the nearby telephone.

"How long have you been gone?" I inquired.

"Three days. Do you miss me?"

"Are you kidding? Finally got this place running right," I declared distractedly, watching, out the window, the dog lead several squirrels, cats and the Archbishop of Canterbury through a complex series of Prussian marching drills.

"I'm coming home tomorrow."

Well, to make a long story short, I had to work round the clock, but the bazooka killed off most of the towels and frightened the dog into submission; the Seabees gave the Archbishop a ride home; and I dumped the sand into the hole where the washing machine had been, so I'm pretty sure she was never the wiser.

And hubba-hubba to you, too, mac.

10

Lost Ann Landers Letter Number Two

DEAR ANN LANDERS: Say a word or two on behalf of us wives of [government nostril inspectors/licensed sausage casing repairmen/wet blasters]. We have had to endure the old stereotype that our husbands are [dirtballs/reptiles/ingenious wax replicas]. I was out to lunch the other day with some [girlfriends/Roman Catholic cardinals/Zulu warriors] and one of them made a cheap and heartless joke about my husband's [breath/DNA/nose bag]. My husband works hard for a dollar, and he is real close to getting one. Also, it is not my fault he married me. How about it, Ann?

—PRICKLY IN PRESCOTT

11

Gender Rolls: My Toilet Seat Problem (and Yours)

Like Marv Throneberry of Lite beer commercial fame, I do not always understand why I have been asked to do something.

For instance, a local college asked me to serve on a discussion panel about the New Man.

The New Man was something nobody had given much thought to at all until, a couple of years ago, the *New York Times Sunday Magazine* did a cover story about a bunch of guys who were concerned with fitness, style, fashion, health, food, furnishings, careers and, above all, with being perceived as genuine, open and sensitive.

The one I remember most vividly from the article was a thirty-two-year-old neurosurgery resident who worked eighty to one hundred hours a week, collected art and cooked for guests at least once a week. I kept wondering how he could do all that and get even five hours of sleep per night. I made a personal vow at that time never to need neurosurgery. I dunno. Maybe art collecting has changed a lot since the last time I checked. They probably have a drive-through window at Christie's now. "Gimme a Modigliani nude, easy on the burnt umber."

I thought the whole idea was, like most of the late twentieth century, a giant media hoax; but I agreed to serve on the panel, mostly because I don't care too much about the actual topics as long as I can, every now and again, glance at my watch and murmur, "Gotta run. I'm serving on a panel tonight."

Then I proceeded to stew about it for weeks on end. The other panelists, I learned, were distinguished educators and such. They would certainly have something to say. I did not.

I thought and thought about the New Man, and I discovered I knew nothing about him. I wasn't even sure whether I had been invited as a critic of the New Man or as an example of him.

"What will you say?" my wife asked me one night.

"I thought I might mention Rousseau."

"What about him."

"I don't know. But one does well to mention Rousseau on panels."

"Well . . ."

"Man in his natural state, right? The social contract?" Actually, I wasn't even sure I had ever read any Rousseau. I considered mentioning instead Frank Russo, a local beauty pageant promoter.

I began to think about the battlegrounds on which gender roles are fought out. You would be surpised at how many of them concern, in some way, where people sit.

Almost from the very moment that anyone thought of sitting on anything, there were problems between men and women. It might be provident to recall, right here, the Birth of Furniture. If someone could just draw the curtain and get the lights, we'll begin.

THE BIRTH OF FURNITURE: AN ANTHROPOLOGICAL PARABLE

(Cue industrial slide show music.)

Shortly after primitive man learned to walk semierect, primitive woman asked if he would mind dragging that rock over there into their cave.

Primitive man wanted to know what for.

To sit on, said primitive woman.

To sit on? In the cave? Who does that? Goes against the whole point of caves, said primitive man. You go in the cave when you're tired of sitting outside on the rocks. You bring the rocks inside the cave, you got nothing to sit on next time you go outside. Next thing, you'll want a tree or a river in the cave.

The couple down the ravine—you know, the ones with the yellow eyes and the big nostrils—have rocks in the cave to sit on, said primitive woman. They have fire too.

Primitive man blinked. They do? Fire? Just burning right there in the cave? That doesn't . . . I mean, don't they. I dunno, just seems kind of dangerous.

About that rock, said primitive woman.

Primitive man wanted to know if it had to be that particular rock, which, he pointed out, was across the gorge and would have to be dragged through a large marsh full of horrible, latching-on kind of bugs the size of Frisbees. (Well, of course, he didn't say "Frisbees." He said, Those smaller, flatter rocks we sometimes throw back and forth for fun, but not for very long and not for very much fun.)

Primitive man added, I could drag in this rock right here beside the cave. Darned nice rock.

No.

No? How come?

Because, said primitive woman, it doesn't go with anything we have.

But we don't have anything, said primitive man.

We have that thing.

Which thing?

The buffalo kind of thing.

Oh, that thing. Well, we'll just get rid of that thing. No problem.

We are not getting rid of the buffalo kind of thing.

How about this rock? primitive man asked, pointing to another one.

No.

No?

See the moss on this rock? asked primitive woman. It's the same color as the moss in our cave.

So it goes with the moss. You said the other one didn't g—

That's too much of that moss color. You need some relief from it. Look, are you going to drag that rock over or are we going to stand here talking until one of those big hammerheaded birds mistakes us for a couple of suet cakes?

Well, gee, said primitive man, I was supposed to go out with the guys. You know, the hunter-gatherers? Tramp around. Hunt. Gather. Have some laughs. Maybe bring something down, boy.

And leave me here with nothing to sit on?

So primitive man went over and got the rock in question and brought it back.

It's not the way I thought it would look, said primitive woman.

What?

It looks different in here. It's . . . bigger. And browner.

So what?

Well, eventually, I kind of envision having a fire over here and some small logs over there. We could store them in the corner . . .

What?

. . . and bring them out when we have people over.

This is a cave! Now, look, the way I understand caves is that they don't have anything in them. That's why they're called caves, see, and if you fill them up, you got no cave.

I don't have the faintest idea what you're talking about.

Well, finally primitive woman found a rock she liked and primitive man moved it into the cave, and things settled down for a while, until one day primitive woman looked up from her ripping—kind of a reverse form of sewing—and said, If I have to look at that rock one more second, I'm going to scream.

This rock? That you had me get?

It's junk. I hate it. It looks like rubble.

It is rubble.

It looks it.

I like it. There's a nice worn-out part for my back and this part that sticks out, so when I pick insects off my leg, I can prop . . .

I hear there's a whole bunch of rocks two valleys over. A big selection.

Good for them.

No, I mean we could go pick one out. They're only there for a limited time. There's a glacier coming or something.

And that was the Birth of Sales. But that's another parable.

(Cue industrial slide show music.)

I hope you all enjoyed that. Could we turn the lights back on? Hey, you, wake up!

Anyway, I decided that the very worst gender role problems have to do with the toilet seat, and I wondered what the New Man would do about it.

Women, as we know, think the toilet seat should be left down after every use.

The Old Man does as he pleases, yes? The New Man would probably like to oblige women, but, as I thought about it, it seemed to me he would be in a tricky spot.

What do women want? In this situation they want the freedom not to look.

Where they're going, I mean. They want, near as I can tell, to be able to hurl themselves blindly at the toilet seat and know they are cleared for a dry landing. No men know exactly why women want this, and most men know better than to ask.

But what if men took the same view (or lack thereof)? That is, what if men decided they shouldn't have to check the seat position before they let fly? What kind of world would it be (Rousseau, op. cit.)? So the New Man must realize that in truckling to the whims of women in this regard, he may be selling out his buddies in church-basement masculinity discussion groups the world over.

Worse still, the New Man, having informed himself on a wide range of subjects, is doubtless aware that Simone de Beauvoir has loaded the toilet seat for bear by suggesting that men, when they pee standing up, mourn for their nursling infancies, for the days when they too sat down to pee. Oh my. Actually I don't believe her. Every so often I try sitting down, like in the old days, and I don't see where it is any great shakes. But if you say you just flatly refuse to believe Simone de Beauvoir, you risk seeming like Rumplestiltskin in the Donahue Age.

With such a great load of subtextual baggage, the toilet seat could not be regarded by the New Man, it seemed to me, with equanimity. Feeling that I was on to something, I headed off to a toilet-seat store to borrow a toilet seat on the very day of the panel discussion. I bumped into my father and mentioned what I was up to.

"Are you sure this is a good idea?" he asked me.

Well, no, but my life has not been dedicated to the pursuit of good ideas. Neither has his. In fact, it seemed kind of unfair of him, after so many decades of the mutual exchange of bad ideas, to start talking suddenly in these terms.

At the bath shop a nicely dressed woman overheard me explaining my plans to the owner and sidled over to me. She told me she had been at a dinner party at which, late in the evening, a little girl had come downstairs, sopping wet in the back. She pointed solemnly at each of the Old American Male guests and said, "Either you . . . or you . . . or you . . ."

This was apparently the end of the anecdote, and I would add, as an aside, that aristocratic people often fail to wrap up their stories quite as decisively as we more lumpen raconteurs might prefer.

This woman then turned to the store owner (herself a woman) and said, "Fortunately I've trained all mine." She could have been talking about ferrets.

This incident burned in my heart and strengthened my resolve to plead the case for a New Man who could exercise some bold new visions, vis-à-vis toilet seats.

That night, at the college, the other panelists had their references to Shakespeare, Fitzgerald, etc.

I had my toilet seat. A toilet seat, detached from its actual toilet (kids, don't try this at home) acquires an added iconographic weight that would surprise the layperson. It suggests the Omega, the Great Mandala, what have you.

I stayed up there awhile illustrating various scenarios. I am not exactly sure what point I wound up making, but a number of women told me afterward they were in the market for exactly that kind of toilet seat. A cannier person—or one prepared to take plastic—would have made a profitable sale then and there.

When I got home, my wife asked, "How did it go?"

"Oh," I said, "you can't go wrong with Rousseau."

12

Case History: The First Pregnant Man

The British magazine *New Society* reported in 1986 that the technology currently exists for a man to give birth. Here now are the words of Guy Ginseng, the Oakland housepainter who volunteered to be the first pregnant man.

I never thought of my body as a temple. It's more of a 7-Eleven. Open at odd hours for cheap, badly planned transactions.

I live in a commune consisting of Alice, a meta-feminist; Kyrie, a Gender-Free Sex Counselor; Max, a linebacker for the 49ers; Veda, a parasexual; and Ernie, a woman who had a transsexual operation to become a man and then discovered that what he really had wanted was to be a tax attorney and is now taking night courses; and me.

We decided to have a child and, after a two-day group meditation, concluded it would be a cop-out if any of the women had it. And Max had a bunch of away games coming up, plus you know how the guys in the locker room would rag him: "Blitzing for two?" That kind of thing.

The biggest problem facing the doctors, as I understand it, was where to put the fertilized egg. I mean you can't just open up the abdomen, drop it in and say, "Write if you get work."

Anyway, the doctors finally decided to install what they call a "cheap uterus." At least that's what I thought they said, and I went along with it because my insurance coverage for this whole thing is a little bit dicey. We've agreed to bill it as a "major G-I series," and if Blue Cross starts asking questions, we'll just say we planned for the kid to join the Army. Anyway, it turns out I didn't hear them right and that they implanted a sheep uterus, which I finally figured out when I'd eaten half the compost heap.

Now I find I really appreciate it when a woman gives up her seat on the bus for me. I'm getting used to the nausea and the heat and the prickling, and the feeling of just being *fat. Fat, fat, fat! I hate this. How could you do this to me?* But I'm ecstatic. I really am. I feel like a man for the first time in my life. If I don't get some Frosty Crunch Swirl ice cream this minute, I'm going to *tear somebody a new navel!*

Also, the mood swings were a problem at first.

13

If God Had Meant for Us to Microwave . . . How in the World Would He Have Let Us Know?

This book urges you to keep technology at arm's length whenever possible, but you will have to become very adept at resisting peer pressure.

Because people who own stupid things become edgy if you don't own one too. Recent microwave oven purchasers are the most dangerous.

"They warm up coffee," these people say, just a little too loudly.

"How nice."

"Leftovers. Leftovers are great." They're almost yelling now. *"Baked potatoes. You have never had such a baked . . ."*

Of course, there is no real reason to own a microwave oven, other than to dump one more hunk of debris into one's own emotional vacuum. It's more a question of faith, like waxy yellow buildup (WYBU). Remember that? A friend and I were reminiscing, rather beerily, about waxy yellow buildup one evening. You don't hear about it anymore, and when my friend mentioned it, I couldn't remember whether it accumulated on one's teeth or ears or clothes or karma.

It is the sort of phrase that could be revived effectively by some glib modern pundit—George Will or somebody. In connection with something like the Iran-Contra mess. "And so it is that the American body politic suffers from a certain waxy yellow buildup, as it were, on the moral touchstone of its . . ." (I'm not sure what a sentence such as this would mean. I'm not even sure what a touchstone is, but you run into them a lot in punditry.)

It would also be a good name for a rock group: Waxy Yellow Buildup. There probably already is one.

My friend remembered that, in sooth, it was supposed to occur on one's floor. And, so the implication went, it would swiftly infect the rest of one's life with negligence and degeneracy.

It was one of those problems that was invented solely to sell the solution. I can't remember the name of the product that was supposed to get rid of waxy yellow buildup—a phrase with considerably more verve and dash than whatever the name of the product was. (One of Madison Avenue's many semiotic misconceptions is the idea that names like Verve and Dash actually *have* verve and dash.)

Anyway, I somehow doubt that we conquered WYBU the way we did cowpox, so I assume that folks just gradually stopped caring about it, in a groundswell of go-with-the-flow, mellow out, *kum-bi-ya* (a Swahili phrase meaning "forget about your waxy buildup which is also yellow, the lion sleeps tonight").

It's almost the same deal with BO, a pungent concern of the sixties. When was the last time you thought about BO? Okay, sure, you run into a whopping case of it now and again, but usually the carrier would never, by dint of advertising, have been persuaded to live his life any other way. The scales are falling from our noses now. BO was never much to write home about, was it?

I feel pretty much the same way about microwave ovens. I don't mean that they cure BO or anything, although, come to mention it, I suppose some large impersonal corporation is experimenting right this minute on helpless bunny rabbits with a microwave deodorizer.

No, what I mean is that when microwave ovens didn't exist, nobody wished for them. Did people sit around (in an emotional vacuum) saying, "Heat is so boring. I wish I could bombard a potato with mutant intergalactic energy. I wish I had a device right here in my kitchen that could alter the known laws of the universe while making French bread pizza, which I also wish existed, in seven seconds."?

Of course not.

So it's a question of faith. You just have to believe that the microwave oven provides you with enough personal enrichment to warrant bringing into your home a phantasmagoric, metamorphosing apparatus that you understand about as well as you understand a subatomic linear supercollider.

I keep waiting for someone to come out with the product that really addresses the issue—an emotional vacuum. "Why be the only one stuck with an emotional vacuum? Give someone this high-strung Voilà! canister model ($86.95 from House of Malezz). It does not clean the floor especially well, but it does keep up a steady stream of mawkishness and pathos the livelong day. A mere touch of the switch gives you: 'Oh, great, wipe the floor with me. No, go ahead, I really enjoy it. Wait. You don't seriously expect me to eat that dust bunny, do you? Hey, do you smell something? Like burning rubber? I'm on fire, aren't I? I'm on fire! Do you know why? *Because you wouldn't change my bag, that's why!* Hey, come back here . . .' "

Someday, for that matter, we will all be encouraged to own some downsized home version of the linear supercollider. Advertising will convince us that we need it. Computers will call us up at home and try to sell it to us (probably reaching, in the process, our answering machines— one of those epiphanic and all-too-rare moments in which two loathsome machines are juxtaposed in such a way that they nullify each other. Huzzah!).

Who is to say what the linear supercollider would do for us? Maybe you could put an orphaned sock into it and cause it to fetch up a matching sock, either the original mate or an analog from another dimension.

I doubt it will do anything so useful. Perhaps it will be the first consumer item whose sole function is to act upon our brains in such a way as to convince us of its necessity.

What a concept. Sweetheart, get me Hammacher Schlemmer.

14

Case History: When Bad Things Happen to Good Potatoes

An illness in the family is one of the most devastating trials any of us will face. In this stunning personal testimony, Glanville Smurl, a Lincoln, Nebraska, oat bran inspector, describes his family's ordeal.

I sure hope she gets better soon because the house isn't the same without her.

When we dropped her off Monday evening, I asked the man if it would be all right if we called the next day, just to see how she was doing.

"Oh sure, we should know something by then," he said.

So I guess it's pretty much touch and go right now.

Our television is broken.

Sure, I know it's stupid to get all worried about an inanimate appliance, but to us, it's more than just an RCA XL-100 television set. It's our link to Bert Convy.

We've had her since she was a newborn, swaddled in

Styrofoam packing, so it came as a blow when we first noticed the trouble brewing. We are not technologically sophisticated people, but we could tell.

"Do you notice anything wrong with the set?" I asked my wife.

"No picture," she said.

Yes, precisely. The sound came on. I could definitely hear Mike Wallace in there talking to me, but the screen was the same sick olive color as it is when the set is off.

"Mike, Mike, I can't see you," I told him.

". . . but isn't this just a gloss on some very tacky slimeball operation which . . ."

"Mike!"

Trying to stay calm, I fell back on my training in Emergency Television Resuscitation, performing the standard four-step process of:

1. Twisting all the controls, one by one, back and forth.
2. Turning the set on and off again.
3. Bracing the set with the left hand, delivering firm slaps with the right hand to various portions of its surface, glancing at the screen after each slap to see if any change has been effected.
4. Keeping warm until members of the National Guard arrive on the scene.

But nothing happened.

I realized that the important thing was to communicate to my wife the need for us to pull together as a united family. So I said to her: "This is your fault! I begged you to get a backup. I told you it couldn't handle the pressure. *Now look what you've . . .*"

But she didn't seem to be hearing me as her pupils slid

up to her forehead and she murmured in a monotone: "No . . . television . . . no . . . telev- . . . slowing down . . . Daisy . . . Dai . . . sy . . . give . . . me . . . your . . . Rosebud."

I believe we both blacked out for a while.

The next day we located the finest specialist that money can buy and brought her in. Now we are just kind of biding our time until we hear something. We have gone thirty-eight hours without a television set, which may be a record for a modern household. I'm going to ask the Guinness people about this when I recover enough motor control to dial a telephone.

In the meantime, my wife and I have had, for the first time in many years, a few nice long talks which, I feel, have done positive things for our relationship. For example, it turns out that her name is not Joyce. That was the name of somebody's wife on television, and I just got a little mixed up. Meanwhile her discovery that I am not the chief of surgery at a large urban hospital has set her mind at ease on the subject of why we don't have more money.

Also, we have experienced some of the standard television-removal phenomena. For example, for the first seven hours after our set left, the glowing face of Larry King hovered in exactly the spot where it would have been had our set still been there. Finally it disappeared, only to be replaced briefly by Sandy Duncan.

On the other hand we have discovered some of the simple pleasures of the past, such as reading aloud to each other. You'd be surprised at how enriching it is just to settle down on the divan and open up a cherished old copy of, say, *TV Guide*.

Me: "Who's the Boss?"—Hilarious complications ensue when Tony mistakes a nuclear breeder reactor for an Asteroids video game.

My wife: "Jake and the Fatman"—Jake disappears mysteriously, causing the Fatman hours of anguished worry until he discovers he has been sitting on him.

After a few hours of this, we are ready to turn in for the night, but not before praying—for this crisis has also shored up certain spiritual values that had gone lax in our home—to Bill Cosby for the healthy recovery of our set.

In the meanwhile we have compromised by hooking the cable up to our food processor. Most of the shows don't come in very well, but if you set it on "CHOP" and squint just a little, "Mr. Belvedere" looks pretty much the same.

15

Boring In on It

If you read between the lines of many self-help books, you will be wasting a lot of time and money, because all you will see is a lot of white space. Still, what I mean to say is that a lot of self-help books wind up looking for euphemistic ways to help people to cope with the fact that they are bored and/or boring.

Scientists have been trying to study boredom ever since the fourteenth century, when it really got to be a problem. The Swiss biologist Prolix de Monotunnus selectively bred boredom into gophers and then examined the brains of the most-bored ones. He was unable to conclude anything at all, and while he was trying to remember what he had been up to in 1345–47, his mother threw out his entire collection of gopher brains.

In many primitive cultures boredom is a prized trait and the most thoroughly bored member of the tribe is revered as a wise man. Among the Langaori of New Guinea, such a man is known as a *hm'd'rm* (trans: he who has noticed that there is not much difference between the pooti bird and the adopu tree. Or between the mika bug and the f'ahoo prawn. Or between the nazuma cat and the . . .).

This raises many tiresome questions about the relation of boredom to historical development. Could a person living in ancient Egypt, centuries before the development of the slide projector and life insurance, have achieved the depth of clinical boredom that is attainable in the modern world?

It seems possible. The third century A.D. Emperor Gaius Tedius was said to be so long and drawn out on the subject of saddle maintenance that he caused the migration of the Jutes and Picts across the land mass of Asia Minor just to avoid hearing him out.

Modern boredom researchers, heroically braving the dangers of handling high-boredom materials all day long, are closer than ever to a cure for boringness, but questions remain about whether the boring could be persuaded to seek treatment.

Many experts believe that tiresome people would acknowledge their affliction only if it entitled them to perks, such as special parking spaces. And then they would go on and on, to whomever would listen, about what a break they were getting.

Still, we can envision a day when we might hear:

"Two for dinner."

"Yes, sir, will that be boring or interesting?"

"Boring, please. Over by the tropical fish tank."

The boring would like that. But they wouldn't want to be called "boring." They would blather ceaselessly about how unfair it was. They would want to be called "charisma impaired" or "personality challenged."

The airline industry stands to benefit tremendously from quantum tedium research. They are already investigating the possibility of seating all the boring people together so that they won't bother the interesting, although it may be even more advantageous to match dull persons with nervous fliers, to make the latter group less jumpy or perhaps less eager to cling to life.

"So I had hard lenses, but they were getting, you know, gunked up with stuff from my eyes, so the optomolotrist said I should get gas, whaddayacallum, gas permanents, but I said since when is there gas in my eyes. Hah! So . . ."

"I see the wing's on fire. Maybe we'll be making a forced landing over water."

"Oh, great, we can share one of those raft deals. So anyway, I got the soft ones, but you have to boil 'em and use one of those, oh, uh, inseam or ecktines cleaner things and . . ."

"That won't be possible. I plan on hurling myself to the sharks."

If I were dull—and maybe I am—I would resent scientific research aimed at making me more interesting. Why should I be classified as the problem? From my point of view, maybe the interesting ones are the problem. With all their bubbly vivacity, they are a nettlesome distraction.

Maybe that's the next thing. Dull Lib. Give me your blah, your humdrum, your listless. Support Your Right to Arm Bores. They'll Take My Dullness Away When They Pry My Cold Dead Fingers off the Actuarial Tables.

What would a Dull Lib rally be like? A lot of people carrying signs that read: "I start flossing at the back of my mouth and work toward the front, but I don't like the extrafine waxed stuff or the new herbal kind because it makes my nose run and . . ."

Who is to say that boringness is not the ideal? And that verve is not the work of the devil? Yes, you could work out a religious argument. Adam and Eve, in their state of perfect innocence, were probably breathtakingly boring.

"How is everything, Eve?"

"Great. Perfect. Wonderful. The persimmons are very tasty. I had a real good kiwi fruit this morning. And the mint is coming up nicely and look over here at the wonderful . . ."

"Nice talking to you."

16

Case History: The Man Who Was Bored by Elvis

Bream Dudgeon, a high school shop teacher from Nondescript, Pennsylvania, reports frequent boring contact with Elvis Presley during the singer's lifetime. He is the author of *Melted Storks,* an unfinished autobiography he started writing and then got sick of.

As the world now knows, I met Elvis in Pittsburgh on October 4, 1963. I was walking home from the library when Elvis, who was performing in town, spotted me from his hotel room. He sent a bodyguard down to fetch me.

He was, it turns out, adding a sun room of some kind to his house and wanted to talk about dry wall and paneling. He set forth his feelings on the subject for two hours and thirty-three minutes.

According to some notes I made after the first encounter, Elvis spoke exclusively about dry wall for the first hour and then eased into paneling. I made several attempts to draw him out on ceiling tiles and was slapped around by the bodyguards for my troubles. After an hour of listening, I experienced some tingling in my scalp, and at two-fifteen elapsed time, I could not feel my fingers.

From that day until his death, Elvis considered me a friend and felt comfortable discussing, at any time of day, any topic that was on his mind.

It was a waking nightmare.

With Elvis I discovered levels of boredom that I can scarcely begin to describe to you. If you imagine your own humdrum, everyday boredoms to be profound, I can only say that it was Elvis's genius to be able to find little crevices in those sorts of boredoms and fill them up with such long-windedness that time seemed to have stopped and the spirit of his listeners would appear to crumble in agonizing slow motion. All of the greatness that Elvis brought to entertainment, he also brought to boring chit-chat.

You should have heard him when he got a food processor. You would have thought he had invented them.

I have been asked by countless authors and tabloid snoops what was Elvis's most boring subject.

I regard that as an offensive question.

How do you compare his three-and-a-half-hour wandering recitation of *every single thing* he could remember from a golf tournament he had watched on television the day before with the seventeen different conversations he initiated with me about a problem he was having with his telephone?

And the food processor. Did I mention the food processor? I did? How about the tennis camp? Oooooo. He took up tennis for a couple of weeks and then went to tennis camp, and he would talk about it like it was *Hanni-*

bal crossing the freaking Alps! Do you have any idea what that's like?

I'm sorry.

But the man was uniquely, incomparably tiresome. It would be sacrilege to engage in comparisons. I hear guys today who are supposed to be boring—your Dukakises, your Jaycee chapter presidents—and I have to say to myself: that's not boring. Sure, it's drab and meaningless, but boring? Not the way I know boring. There was only one King.

My only regret was that he did not have grandchildren. Can you imagine what he would have done with grandchildren?

17

It Is Meat and Right

My wife and I struck our dietary reef on the night we watched that infamous "60 Minutes" broadcast wherein it was established that the your average chicken, before it reaches your average grocer's meat cooler, is chained to the back of a '73 Buick and dragged through the streets of Paterson, N.J.

Or was that Andy Rooney?

Actually the Buick was one of the more sanitary methods for readying the chickens. In other cases they were . . . they showed . . . actually, my memory is a little hazy about this because I went into a mild swoon around the time they . . . showed . . . there was . . . this vat of . . . never mind.

Basically if you had offered me a choice of watching this thing about the chicken plants or watching a forty-minute special about the surface of Harry Reasoner's tongue or watching any television program involving Geraldo Rivera, I would have said, "Bring on Harry's papillae."

But that's just my way.

Later that evening, as soon as my wife and I were able to sit upright and take a little tea and toast, one of us said, "Woooo. Let's stop eating meat."

So we did.

That was years ago, and I have not purchased one scrap of meat for our household since, except for what the dogs eat. The dogs, by the way, eat something called Eukanuba, a scientifically balanced designer dog food that retails for roughly the same unit price as Swiss Water Process Decaffeinated Sun-Dried Tomato-and-Duck-Flavored coffee beans.

So every night we sit down to a groaning table piled high with steamed chickpea stems and corn melba, while the dogs wallow on the floor eating desiccated porterhouse steak.

For a while we even tried to follow the American Heart Association guidelines, which are: for every thousand calories consumed each day, you should take in no more than three hundred cubits of cholesterol and no more than three silver talents of sodium, with saturated fats comprising no more than 10 percent; and in the event of a tie, home records and class participation will be considered for those whose medical expenses exceed 5.7 percent of adjusted gross income, dealer prep and licensing not included.

Looks simple enough on paper, but when you try to apply it to your life, it gets a little confusing.

A sample day of eating under those guidelines included:

BREAKFAST

1 slice lo-flavor sprouted thistle bread, toasted and left to cool
1/2 cup unsweetened pine husks
1 glass melba gourd juice
seaweed cobbler
baby radishes
2 cups coffee helper

LUNCH

Filbert and tangerine sandwich on semitoasted Latvian flat bread
baby radishes
kasha tots
mackerel cobbler
grasshopper (not the drink, the bug)

SNACK

1 stick, 5 to 7 inches long (choice of hickory, birch, larch)

DINNER

blackened raisins
eggplant melba
baby radish cobbler
tofu whiskey (up to three glasses)

The advantages of such a diet are obvious:

1. It contains a lot of sharp, jagged things that could conceivably ream out your system so as to dislodge the Hostess Sno Balls, which you ate during the Johnson Administration and which have been clinging to your insides and possibly even gathering themselves for some kind of charge, and which will probably be around, bright and pink as ever, long after the very last speck of plutonium in the universe has degraded into compost. (N.B. Some research suggests that forced removal of a severely impacted Sno Ball could jeopardize the so-called "host organism," so proceed with caution.)
2. If you eat this way for a few days, you will cry a lot, lowering your sodium count and making it possible for you to return sooner to your old diet, which was heavy on xanthium bean gum and Slim Jims.
3. A really concerted effort by Americans to eat baby radishes has the potential to exhaust the entire radish supply, ridding our land of this troublesome pest for the foreseeable future.
4. Foods whose names contain the world "melba" are invariably good for you and not very tasty. They are all imported from the Melba Islands, which get virtually no rainfall, sunshine or wind.

After giving it our very best shot for about a day and a half, my wife and I cast aside the guidelines and simply tried to partake responsibly of the Four Major Food Groups: the Root Group, the Chip Group, the Pudding Group and the Liquor Group. (Speaking of the Liquor Group, recent studies have indicated, gratifyingly, that a drink or two may actually be beneficial in certain respects. Some people have interpreted this rather creatively as an endorsement of their lifestyles. Two indications that you are exceeding healthy limits for alcohol intake are: (a) if people are frequently under the mistaken impression that you are doing your Crazy Googenheim impersonation and (b) if you routinely wake up in Midwestern bus stations dressed as an ostrich, having missed more than one major holiday.)

At the present time it would not be quite true to say that my wife and I are vegetarians.

For one thing we eat fish. We reasoned that—unlike commercial livestock, which are often penned up and force-fed antibiotics and growth hormones (or was that Andy Rooney?)—fish are allowed to roam freely through the ocean waters, eating hospital wastes until their little hearts burst with joy.

And should you invite us to your house—a gesture which, assuming you paid for this book, I am not in any way counting on—we would eat what was served. If you put some ribs in front of me right now, I would eat them, provided you could establish that they came from a relatively mainstream animal.

Also we have kind of an open marriage, meatwise. When we are not at home, each of us makes his or her own personal decision about whether or not to eat meat.

This is mostly for the sake of my wife. My wife is a slim person of modest appetite, but she is also from Iowa, where meat is venerated in much the way that people in primitive cultures worship Richard Gere. People in Iowa keep photo albums containing cherished pictures of especially memorable roasts they have eaten over the years.

So periodically my wife will announce that she is getting "anemic" or "iron-deficient" or "hypoglycemic."

These are all sophisticated medical terms which, if I had to render them in crude layman's speech, might come out as "Me want meat." In point of fact, my wife could probably feel iron-deficient several minutes after eating an anvil.

I know that my wife's Midwestern background sometimes overwhelms her and obliges her to eat meat for lunch. I know this not because she tells me but because I occasionally notice, in the back of her Datsun, a McDonald's bag or the stripped skeleton of a longhorn steer.

So I was none too surprised when a study was released in late 1987 claiming that Americans were eating roughly the same amount of meat as they had been four years earlier but were having more trouble admitting it.

The study was paid for by the American Meat Institute —I always wonder how their offices are decorated—and the National Live Stock and Meat Board. Cynical beast that I am, I caught myself wondering if they would have rushed into print if the figures had, perish the thought, gone the other way.

A BRIEF REBUTTAL

The Meat Outlook Organization (MOO) has asked for equal time in this book to answer some of the comments made above. Out of respect for the fine work this group has done to promote physical fitness, including the construction of a lap pool right here on my property, I have consented.

Are you part of the New Beef Generation? Beef keeps you alert and helps you relax. Increasingly Americans are turning to beef as their new energy and success food.

Here are some common myths about beef, many of them circulated by Communists and subversives.

Myth No. 1: Cows Do Not Enjoy Becoming Beef

Yes, in the old days of the so-called slaughterhouse, this was true. Thank goodness the slaughterhouse is now a thing of the distant past. Today's cows are brought to a Cattle Life Awareness Center, where, for a period of up to six weeks, they are counseled and helped to see their role in the food chain.

Bovine counselors run encounter groups at which each cow is challenged about some of its closely held assumptions. There are trust exercises, in which the cow falls sideways and relies on others to catch it. Martial arts classes in *tae kow do* (Okinawan for "empty hooves") help the cows grow in confidence and body awareness.

"When they first come in here, they're fighting the whole idea," relates Win Thalia, a cownselor at North Dakota Cowspice. "As the days pass, though, you can see the change in their eyes."

Terms like "slaughter" and "butcher" have been struck from the cattleman's lexicon. The New Cow is brought to the destructuring area where, in the parlance of the era, it "cashes in its chips."

"It's a beautiful thing to see an animal so at one with its meatness," Thalia says.

You can taste the fulfillment.

Myth No. 2: Beef Just Sits There in Your Stomach and Makes You Feel Awful

Maybe in the days before Enzymatically Predigested Lite Beef this was true. Today you have no more trouble digesting the New Beef than a lion would have digesting Cheerios.

The busy professional who can't afford to get filled up will enjoy Hoofer's Time Release Delmonico Packets, which send steady bursts of protein and soothing endorphins to the brain, just when you need them most to keep your act together in the competitive and carnivorous business world.

Myth No. 3: Beef Is Bad for You

Now does that make a lick of sense? Look at cows. They are full of beef, but when was the last time you heard of a cow having a heart attack? Besides, could something as sweet and placid as a cow mean you any harm? 'Course not.

But like so many of nature's gifts—sugar, salt, lightning, hydrochloric acid—beef must be approached with some thought of moderation.

A study conducted by the Institute for Expensive Privately Funded Studies in Largesse, Maryland, established that it is perfectly safe to stuff yourself with a big, red, dripping, outwardly charred T-bone steak ribboned with delicate lodes of moist fat, provided you follow it up with balancing meals of kale, sesame bran and spring water. For approximately the next year and a half.

And never forget: we are on the threshold of a New Beef Frontier.

The industry is hard at work on innovations such as Anti-Steak, a magic-bullet substance capable of counteracting every single effect of beef if consumed within ten minutes after the meal in question. And then there's the Cattle Reef Project, where cows are being bred to live and breathe underwater and thus acquire the many healthful aspects of fish.

So whether you're on the go, at the beach, or reading a nasty, seditious little book like this one, have some beef! It's good for you, America.

SOME BARBECUING TIPS

It's funny how life works out sometimes. No sooner did the lap pool guys leave than I began thinking about how great it would be if I had a water slide that went right out my bedroom window and into the pool. Huh? Wouldn't that be great. I just happened to mention this idea over lunch with a couple of lobbyists from the Charcoal Briquette Institute for the Public Good, and they said, what a coincidence, they just happened to, etc., etc. —you get the picture. Anyway, all I have to do is answer a few public-service type questions about barbecuing and I get my water slide. (Do you suppose someone like Flaubert ever cut these kinds of deals? "Look, Gustave, just stick in a scene where Emma opens up a can of Ennui-brand snails, and we'll pick up all your dental bills . . .")

Q: Is it healthy to eat a lot of barbecued meat?
A: Depends on what you mean by "a lot." It's like anything else. Four or five Good and Plentys a day consti-

tute a sensible and healthful dietary supplement, but if you eat, say, forty-eight boxes of them in a couple of hours, you will lapse into a coma and your body will begin blinking pink-*white*-pink-*white* and the people from the emergency helicopter will say to your loved one, "I'm afraid we're going to have to tie that sucker to the landing runner, ma'am, being as we don't allow blinking radioactive folks in the fuselage per se."

What was I talking about?

Ah, barbecued meat. Obviously, if your family of four finds itself going through a whole candied yak every couple of days, you have to ask yourself two very hard questions:

1. Is this too much barbecued meat?
2. Who are these other three people? I thought I lived alone.

Barbecue positivists note that barbecued meat can't be all that bad for you, inasmuch as primitive humans lived almost exclusively on it.

This is not quite true. The most primitive humans had no idea how to light a fire. When they wanted to barbecue, they had no choice but to wheel their Weber grill out of the cave and sit there waiting for lightning to strike it, which often took years, the beer got warm, etc.

Also, primitive man lacked the reasoning power to plan a barbecue. He generally told people to "bring a dish," and everyone would show up with potato salad. Twenty-three *Pithecanthropi erecti* standing around twenty-three bowls of potato salad. And the potato salad was awful then. Had rocks and swampy stuff in it.

Q: How often should I clean the surface of my grill?

A: It hardly matters what I say, because you won't ever clean it, will you? Nobody does.

The disgusting material that builds up on the rungs of the grill is properly known as "ptoo." (Its closest molecular cousin is the disgusting black stuff that builds up on the undersides of cars during the winter and cannot be removed by anything less authoritative than a bazooka. That stuff is called "zigg," in case anybody asks you.) Scientists have begun to study ptoo only recently, and research has proceeded slowly, due to the tendency of microscopes to explode when slides of this highly unstable material are inserted.

"Chances are, if we could, whaddyacallit, inertify it, it would turn out to be a cure for something, I expect," said a man named Bill who answered the phone at the National House o' Science in Bethesda, Maryland.

There are those, however, who argue that ptoo represents a new—if not particularly charming—life-form. These assertions are somewhat shored up by the claims of Mr. and Mrs. Trumaine "Pee Wee" Willibald of Extra Cheese, Alabama.

The Willibalds say a UFO landed in their backyard and a large fluorescent spider—except it had five legs, and in the middle where the body would be there was just a chimpanzee's face—got out and began to converse excitedly with the ptoo on their grill. The two of them went on and on, say the Willibalds, who could not get a word in edgewise.

Q: What's the best way to get charcoal going good?

A: Good question. And yet a better way to look at it might be to ask: of all the dagblasted things in the world, why do we have to cook over something as pyrotechnically uncooperative as charcoal?

What is charcoal, anyway? I'm not sure exactly, but I think it's safe to say it is something that has been burned and then some. (I apologize for getting into technological jargon here. "Burned and then some" is a scientific term referring to a substance whose total mass has been raised to a temperature of 2,890 degrees Fahrenheit + HRT, with HRT representing the temperature of Harry Reasoner's tongue.)

That's why charcoal is so hard to set on fire. It has already *been* on fire. It's all *through* burning. It resents being asked to burn one more time. It's ready to move on now to the next phase of the great carbon chain of life: festering. You would have more luck getting *beach sand* to catch fire.

But to answer the question, I guess I recommend dousing the charcoal with something flammable, like New Jersey rainwater or the coffee you get at work. But if it gets on the ptoo, contact your local civil defense officials.

18

Eating Cro- (Magnon)

Okay, so are we saying forget about diets? Not necessarily. For example, I read recently about a diet called
"The Paleolithic Prescription," based on the idea that
we'd be healthier if our lifestyles more closely resembled
those of the Cro-Magnon hunter-gatherers who roamed
the earth forty thousand years ago. No, wait. To say they
"roamed" may be a Cro-Magnon ethnic stereotype. Quite
frequently they knew where they were going.

SAMPLE CRO-MAGNON CONVERSATION

First guy: "Where're you going?"
Second guy: "Back to the, ah, . . . the place where
they've got, ah, got, oh, . . . mossy skins of some kind
stretched (muffled) stretched across some . . . It's not
strictly a lean-to, I wouldn't say . . . but although I am
not personally privy to every interpretation of the frame-
work . . ."

No, wait. That was not entirely a sample Cro-Magnon conversation.

Anyway, the theory of "The Paleolithic Prescription" —from what I've been able to ascertain by looking out the window and imagining what it would have been like to have done some serious research—is that our bodies are still pretty much designed for the diet and exercise regimen of a hunter-gatherer life. So you shouldn't eat things that you wouldn't have been able to hunt or gather. Now, let's try this again.

SAMPLE CRO-MAGNON CONVERSATION

First guy: "You hunting or gathering today?"

Second guy: "Gathering."

First guy: "Again with the gathering. You didn't gather yesterday? It would kill you to hunt a little?"

Second guy: "I'm on a little roll with the gathering. Is that so bad?"

First guy: "What're you gathering today?"

Second guy: "Ben and Jerry's Heath Bar Crunch Ice Cream."

First guy: "How's it going?"

Second guy: "Not so good. Doesn't seem to be any. I checked over by the . . . where the, ah, rock sticks out . . ."

Anyway, your hunter-gatherers ate what they could get. An average daily menu might consist of:

1 bunch loose stalks

4 berries partly smushed

3 tubers, semievolved, left on a rock preheated to 350 degrees, for one hour

1/2 cup leftover mastodon tetrazzini

1 greenish-red thing, not quite sure what it was

Right there you notice one of the big drawbacks of Paleolithic dining—you had to eat a lot of stuff you couldn't be too sure about. In each case, somebody had to be the first guy ever to eat one.

"Guys? You know these things? I'm going to take a shot at eating one."

"All right! Go for it, Jimmy."

"Whoo, looks like that was a mistake."

I suppose something of the same uncertainty must attach itself to the people who test modern comestibles. Someone had to be the first person to eat Donkey Kong cereal.

Of course, the hunter-gatherers also got loads of exercise. Just being alive was a big exercise. Sample daily workout routine for them would be:

- Being generally afraid—2,000 calories
- Being specifically afraid of something charging right at you and salivating—8,000 calories
- Scratching—100 calories
- Solar eclipse (pointing at, yelling, clutching head and hopping)—3,000 calories
- Racquetball—400 calories

That last one was a joke. Cro-Magnon man did not play racquetball, because his crude thought processes could not accommodate the requisite level of self-involvement and because he couldn't afford the court fees.

Many of you may be saying right now, "Hey, wait a second, this is no Tom Clancy book. Somebody musta switched the dust jackets."

Still others, however, may be saying: "What good is this Paleolithic wheely-dealy? As a respected member of the community and an officer in the Elks, I cannot be expected to grub around in people's yards and leap from the trees onto small animals and scrabble around in a state of wild-eyed ferocity. Well, not counting right after big sales meetings."

You make a good point, respected member of the community. But your society has provided you with another means to replicate the pulse-quickening excitement felt by primitive man as he scampered across a threatening terrain, beset by predators and buffeted by strange environmental forces.

The supermarket.

Please proceed in an orderly fashion, single file, to the next chapter.

19

What to Do in the Supermarket, Part One

Yes, the supermarket is the modern analog to those frightening food-gathering venues of Cro-Magnon yore.

I was standing in the supermarket checkout line one day some time ago; and, as I so often do, I began browsing through the *Reader's Digest* to numb the nameless dread surging up through my sternum.

Lo, there was, right near "I Am Joe's Sternum," an article titled "Never Be Nervous Again."

My interest quickened. I was pretty darn nervous right then, mostly because I was wrestling with some anticipatory dread regarding Vegetable Recognition Deficit Disorder, a disease that strikes nine out of thirteen supermarket checkout persons.

If you are worried that you may have contracted VRDD, check yourself for the four early warning signs:

1. You are working in a supermarket.
2. A vegetable, carried along on the conveyor belt, arrives in front of you.

3. You don't know what it is.

4. A crusty patch appears on your skin or scalp.

Actually, number four is not one of the early warning signs of VRDD. I just had a sudden urge to mention something kind of disgusting.

VRDD is one of those diseases—like halitosis or joining the Jaycees—that cause more problems for other, nearby people than for the afflicted person.

Here is what happens to me when I encounter a VRDD sufferer: The checkout person will pick up, say, a bunch of kohlrabi and frown at it. Then he (or she) will give me a heavy-lidded look.

"What is this?"

"Kohlrabi."

"It doesn't look like broccoli."

"No, kohlrabi."

Another heavy-lidded look. I am getting nervous. Suddenly I am a guy who likes strange vegetables. The bagger has picked up the scent and is staring at me too.

The checker inspects the little plastic-covered card by the register where all the produce prices are listed. Except, somehow, all of the listings are for "Beans." Beans, certain kind—79 cents a pound. Beans, other kind—69 cents a pound. Beans, don't know what kind—89 cents a pound.

"I don't have a price for this," the checker says, a little sullenly.

Now there hangs in the air a powerful suspicion that I have smuggled into the store some kind of mutant, unwholesome Hungarian vegetable with the twisted intention of discussing it with an attractive underaged person. I feel even more like a misfit than I ordinarily do. I glance down at the kohlrabi and, yes, it has begun to look strangely lewd.

A manager is summoned. At twenty-three, she is wise in the ways of the world and has been instructed in how to humor spiritually and psychologically disadvantaged persons.

"How much do *you* think the 'kolaberwati' costs?" she asks sweetly, trying to thrust responsibility for the whole sordid episode back into my clammy, tuber-fondling hands.

Eventually I am allowed to slink out to my car with my loathsome cargo.

With the prospect of this messy debacle stretching out before me, you can well understand why I paged frantically through "Never Be Nervous Again" with the idea of locating some gleaming smidgen of hope.

I scanned the article, and I read, "You've been invited to a big dinner party in two weeks. You know that one of the other guests is a politician."

I have? I do? No, wait, it was just a hypothetical scenario. This was supposed to make me *less* nervous? Why *don't* I get invited to big dinner parties with politicians? Is it because of my vegetable fetish?

The article's author, one Dorothy Sarnoff, went on to suggest that I could feel less nervous if I learned to contract the muscles that lie just below where my ribs begin to splay. (My *ribs* are splaying? Ooog.) She calls this area the "vital triangle."

Could I just say something about the vital triangle? It often seems as though nary a day passes without mention, in the media, of a new zone or spot somewhere on one's person. As thinking, feeling individuals, we are encouraged to (a) discover these places on ourselves and

(b) elicit some response from them, possibly with the assistance of an outside party.

It's almost a full-time job. I have begun to picture myself as something akin to those maps of a cow showing all the cuts of beef. There is almost no space left on my body that has not been identified by some self-help guru as being rife with possibilities for pulsation or manipulation of some kind, usually with the goal of inducing a spasm. I'm a reasonable man, and I can see that there's nothing wrong with a spasm here, a spasm there. But many of today's self-help books conceive of the well-lived life as nothing more than one enormous *fit*. You won't get that kind of treatment here in this book. I want you to feel free to think of yourself as mostly inert flesh, unencumbered by the potential for greater fulfillment.

Anyway, as my prospective purchases drew ever closer to the cashier, I searched desperately for my vital triangle. I located an anatomical nebula which I assumed to be the object of my quest, but I was unable to make it contract. I believe there was something lodged in one of my rib splays.

I believe it was a piece of kohlrabi.

20

What to Do in the Supermarket, Part Two

On a more recent evening I was again standing in the supermarket, this time in the express checkout line.

I was buoyed, supercharged with confidence in myself, because I had, without any premeditation, arrived at the registers with *exactly* twelve items, the legal limit for express.

This was also achieved without any fudging. You will run into some people who squinch together three or four identical cans of Pope Tomato Paste or Mighty Dog Liver 'n' Beef in the configuration of an Audi grill ornament on the black conveyor belt, as if to suggest that, by dint of sheer interchangeability, these three or four cans represent only one item in the express count.

I have to say to you people, hey, wake up and smell the chamomile! Where would this kind of logic end? How would you like it if I showed up in front of you with twelve groupings, each one a set of twenty-five identical cans and each therefore representing, in your heretical antinomian doctrine, a single unit of commerce. I'd have

—I just roughed this out—three hundred items! In the express line! Geez!

(I have always wanted to mention—and this is as good a time as any—my unbounded admiration for an Italian tomato company with the—I suppose "chutzpah" is absolutely the wrong word—with the "pluck" to call itself Pope. There is no getting around the implications, especially right in the guy's backyard, of greatness, infallibility and apostolicity. By the way, has anyone handling the Pope advertising account considered the presence, in the word "apostolicity," of the sound "pasta"? Way to go, Pope. Say what you will, I doubt there is a Tibetan chutney bottler with the brand name "Dalai.")

From a public-policy standpoint, I have always felt that twelve was really too high for an express limit anyway. With twelve you can often solve the immediate, pressing problems of your life, plus indulge in a few whims, go off on tangents. Express should be like Ollie North: lean, mean and purposeful. The Bush people would do well to look into this matter as part of their legislative package. (I mean the George Bush people, not the bush people who scratch out an existence on the cruel Kalahari and rarely *own* twelve separate items at one time.)

On the other hand, as any serious student of supermarket traffic flow well knows, the sheer number of items plays a relatively small role in determining the speed of a line. That is, the difference between fourteen items and twenty-four will not weigh as heavily in the outcome as:

1. The presence (or absence) of a bagger keeping pace with the flow of items (although it should be noted that many baggers consider it a point of matadorial insouciance and panache to let a couple

of bags worth of items build in front of them before actually setting to work).

2. The number of different customers ahead of you. Two customers buying ten items each will take up a greater aggregate block of time than a single customer buying as many as thirty-five items. Generally speaking.

3. The question of whether the customer(s) ahead of you will pay by check or cash. Check transactions, with their attendant layer of paperwork and verification, are vastly more time-consuming, especially because many check writers do not use their time profitably to fill out most of the check. Such factors as the date, the purchaser's name and that of the store are unlikely to change while the merchandise is being rung up. Get on the stick, you check writers.

(Speaking of sticks, does anything hark more directly back to our Cro-Magnon ancestors than that stick we place between our purchases and those of someone else? It is tantamount to urinating on one's property to demarcate it, a practice not condoned among humans, except in certain parts of Wisconsin. And there is a tricky question of etiquette, too. It is considered gallant, from what I can discern, for the person whose stuff is being rung up to place the stick at the tail end of his or her purchases, thus inviting the next person to use belt space as it becomes available. In the absence of such a gesture, though, the person waiting may reach forward and . . . ah, who cares?)

Of all of these considerations, the first is the most piquant and double-edged because many of us are happy to welcome the sight of a bagger speeding up the process for the customers ahead of us but would prefer, when our own time comes, to bag our groceries.

We all have our crank theories. Mine is the Cumulative Refrigerative Effect ("frigidus totus in sackum unum"). I hold that putting all the cold stuff in one bag accomplishes a lot more than slipping one cold item in a little plastic sub-bag and dropping it in among a bunch of room-temperature items. If you don't believe me . . . I dunno, there's probably some nifty little home experiment you could devise, but I haven't got the patience to think of it just now.

But the more gigantic importance of bagging your own groceries is that it gives you the opportunity to avoid —without having to importune some mystified VRDD-bedeviled clerk—those newly fashionable large plastic bags, which—are you listening, wicked supermarket barons?—*nobody likes.*

It goes without saying that they are disgusting environmental menaces and have contributed to our current atmospheric predicament, which is to say, we would all be a lot more comfortable as life-forms if we moved to Pluto.

But let us consider these bags *qua* bags. The really critical moments in any grocery bag's life are (1) being picked up and (2) being put down. I think we can all agree that these bags fail miserably in both respects.

1. When picked up, plastic bags function like those tiger traps you see on old jungle movies, where the tiger walks over the net and the ropes yank him up in the air, but instead of a tiger, what gets yanked up is your jar of Tuscan peppers and Zeus chips and Philadelphia cream cheese and bran muffins, all smushing and crushing each other.
2. Putting down a shapeless, amoeboid plastic grocery

bag is comparable to cutting down the tiger trap. The tiger scrambles out. Your stuff has no incentive to stay in one of those plastic bags. How many of us have put one down on the floor of a car and then, three weeks later, found a decomposed kiwi fruit that went MIA and rolled down by the manifold?

To spare myself the ordeal of explaining this rationale to a supermarket employee, I try to bag my own stuff whenever possible. But in the express line on the night in question, I encountered—as one does more and more these days—one of those new setups where a bagging shelf has been installed right in front of the cashier's waist, so that only a personal-space invader on the order of Morton Downey, Jr., could possibly bag his own groceries.

This is made possible, in ergonomic theory, by the red goblin light that reads the bar codes. Wicked supermarket barons, I defy you to find a free-thinking person who trusts those goblin lights to be accurate or to speed up the process, particularly since the clerk frequently waves your package of corn Niblets over the goblin hole five or six times, eliciting a multitude of beeps and boops and causing you to wonder how many corn Niblets you would see listed if you looked at the receipt, which you hate to do right then and there for fear of seeming niggling and accusatory. Plus there's the whole question of whether goblin rays mutate your corn Niblets.

Yet as I stood there in line on this night in question, I found in myself a comforting sense of fellowship with the other supermarket patrons. We shared a vast befuddlement at the pass to which things had come. And the supermarket was briefly transmogrified in my eyes into a Great Mandala on which we all rode out our destinies of unasked-for goblin lights and plastic bags.

I decided I would find some way to exchange greetings with one of my consumerist comrades, in the manner in which the Peace is exchanged at many church services. I turned to the woman behind me, and, beaming with Paleolithic bonhomie, I searched for a way to share my feelings with her. I noticed that she had only one purchase: a road atlas.

The monumental absurdity of it washed over me, and I blurted to her, "Did you ever think, years ago, that you would someday say, 'I'm going to dash out to the grocery store for . . . a road atlas?' "

This missed the mark in some way. She gave me one of those get-out-of-my-aura looks that one gets all too frequently nowadays. Still, a self-help-book writer should know enough to realize that not everyone will be ready to share a supermarket Cro-Magnon epiphany at exactly the same moment. Anyway, I may have caught her right in the middle of contracting her vital triangle.

21

Grub

A person will ingest any number of bugs in a lifetime. I suppose that's a pretty unpromising way to begin a chapter, but there is no denying hard facts. Like the Trilateral Commission, Jack Kemp, microwaves and the Elks, bugs are out there, and every once in a while, one goes up your nose or slips into your mouth.

When you were very young and less distinct from the rest of the universe, this happened a lot, and you did not care. This is worth bearing in mind, because bugs may be coming back as a food trend.

I read that University of Wisconsin entomologist Gene DeFoliart believes that insects are an important food source. DeFoliart himself, the article alleged, will scarf down the occasional handful of deep-fried greater wax moth larvae.

I have always felt it is a bad idea to dip into one's scientific inventory for snacks. It's a good thing that Gene does not study condors, given this predilection of his. I also wonder if any of Gene's students, after handing in a lab study of Mormon cricket livers, has had to go home and inform the family dog, "My professor ate my homework."

DeFoliart believes that bugs are going to catch on with hungry folks. "Insects are the most protein available to people who don't have anything else" was how he put it. I think you'd want to have a marketing firm punch that slogan up a little bit before you went national with it. Maybe turn it into "When you have nothing else, nothing else but a bug will do."

The article on DeFoliart does not delve into his personal life, but it crossed my mind that he may have trouble getting women (or anyone) to kiss him, especially as he goes more public with his entophagia. "Yeah, Gene, but exactly how recently did you eat one? Are we talking a day, a week, or what?" (Readers of my first book, *Swimming Chickens*—those five or six who did not subsequently swear off reading altogether—may find themselves remembering Nick Kotula, the bachelor who acquired a reputation for flushing live bats down his toilet and then discovered that women would not visit his home for any great length of time because they were afraid to use the bathroom.)

I'd like to be a (pretty much invisible) fly on the wall at one of DeFoliart's dinner parties. I bet there is an undercurrent of edginess. "So, Gene, great risotto. What exactly is in it? Not that I . . . I mean, I just assume you wouldn't . . . Gene?"

Of course, it's not a brand-new idea. You got your John the Baptist, for one. Locusts and honey never sounded so bad to me. Given a choice of honey-glazed locusts done to a nice turn and any of the various chicken crypto-nuggets on the market, I believe I would say, "Pass them hoppers." The monotony, I guess, was part of the hardship for John. I imagine he had any number of days when he was tempted to send out for dragonflies and hard sauce, just for a little variety.

[Reader Alert! We are entering one of those brief, unfortunate stretches where some real, legitimate knowledge has somehow slipped into this book.] Actually, about five hundred varieties of insects are eaten in Asia, Latin America, Africa and Ohio. In Mexico water bug eggs are harvested as a kind of jiminy caviar; and immature ants (called "escamoles") are considered a delicacy, which probably puts a lot of pressure on Mexican ants to grow up fast. None of this Michael Jackson stuff.

As grazing land grows scarce and the ozone layer depletes and Geraldo Rivera does increasing numbers of prime-time specials and life degenerates imperceptibly into savagery, insect eating will probably make a heck of a lot of sense, which will be a great joke on the insects, who have been waiting patiently for us to die out so they can take over the world (a scenario documented impressively by helpful movies like *The Hellstrom Chronicle,* which prompted resentful humans to roam the streets hunting butterflies with staple guns).

I'm just wondering whether I should start gearing up to issue my own line of bug munchies before someone else trademarks John the Baptist as a brand name. I'm already way out in front in the insect husbandry department. When it comes to punching them six-legged dogies, my yard is the high chaparral, podner. (This is going to make an interesting Budweiser commercial. "For all the guys who rope the flies and brand the gnats . . .")

My pea patch, for instance, is currently kind of a transitional neighborhood. It could go pea patch, or it could go beetle amusement park with a subtle pea theme. I'm not even sure what kind of beetles these are. I may have discovered a new species, in which case, I plan to name them after Warren Beatty, since I have never, ever encountered them when they weren't locked into a double-cheese-burger position. They seem to be able to conduct all of their business and eat my pea vines without ever disengaging from one another. I'm not sure anyone, except maybe the wasted, anarchical young thrill seekers in *Less Than Zero,* would want to eat this particular insect.

Still, the crunch profile is great, and the focus groups loved them on the French bread pizzas, so . . .

22

Smart Cookies / Loose Fillings

Many of you out there may be experiencing loss of appetite, skin pallor, lack of energy and a general feeling of restlessness. While it is possible that you have done nothing more harmful than watch C-SPAN for extended periods, you should know that these are also symptoms of Post-Girl-Scout-Cookie-Distribution Stress Syndrome.

The syndrome manifests itself in five ways:

1. *Overdose.* Many people simply do not believe that Girl Scout cookies are, in the strictest sense, cookies. They may "know" this intellectually, but on some deeper level they feel that common-sense principles for safe cookie consumption do not apply to Girl Scout cookies.

   Some theorists speculate that this is because these cookies represent a peculiar area in which public spiritedness and gluttony overlap.

   If you come upon someone who has overdosed on Girl Scout cookies, *do not try to move him.* You'll only strain yourself. Keep him warm or cold, as the case may be, until trained confection-control personnel arrive. Also count the number and note the color of empty boxes around the victim. If split-second decisions have to be made at the hospital, it is helpful to know whether it was four boxes of Scot-Teas (a "quadruple bagpipe" in hospital slang) or five of Savannahs (the so-called "Surrender at Appomaalox").

2. *Post-Gorging Despair.* No matter how many boxes of these cookies a user orders, there doesn't ever seem to be any in the house two or three days after the delivery. It is not uncommon for someone to eat her entire allotment of Thin Mints in a day and a half, and then see the rest of the year stretching out before her, all 363½ days of it, bleak and mintless.

Flavia H: "I didn't see how I could go on. I quit the Sweet Adelines, broke off my engagement to Dwayne and hocked most of the letters in my last name to buy one box on the green market."

Many communities have set up sharing groups for these shattered spirits. These groups meet in church basements, take field trips to supermarkets and bakeries and hold educational seminars on responsible cookie use.

"Our motto is 'There are no *bad* cookies, only no *more* cookies,'" explains Waldo Gideon, chief interlocuter for the Weatogue Sharing Group.

3. *Blanche DuBois Disorder.* It is a fact of life that Brownies sell the most cookies because they are cuter. For many older Girl Scouts, this comes as a brutal shock. For the first times in their lives, they must acknowledge that, even at the age of nine or

ten, their charms are already fading. Many of them acquire Southern accents, begin smoking and drinking heavily, and constantly complain that the uniform makes them look matronly.

A group of cadets who feel they have broken through this syndrome and reached the other side have published the book *Our Sashes/Ourselves: A Meta-Cookie Manifesto,* available at better bookstores.

4. *Willie Loman Disorder.* In today's competitive world, it is more and more common to find parents helping their daughters write up cookie orders in the parents' workplace. This creates enormous pressure for the coworkers of said parents. In many cases, coworkers who live alone on straitened incomes are nonetheless obliged to buy sixteen or seventeen boxes of cookies, just to placate everyone at the office.

On the plus side, surplus boxes can be stored and sold at a considerable markup outside church basements where Post-Gorging Despair Sharing Groups are meeting.

5. *Letdown.* More and more, cookie therapists encounter people who suffer from a generalized sense of depression and vague feelings that the cookies aren't as good as they used to be. With this in mind the Center for Girl Scout Cookie Research has been funded to brainstorm new cookies that speak to the spirit of the times.

Some cookies on the drawing board:

• *First Nancies.* White sequins dot the smooth, inviting strawberry-red coating, but inside is a hard, resistant center. A glamorous, but—and never forget this—tough cookie.

- *Barbarabusherellas.* White and wispy and plump, not a sweet cookie for late-night snacks, but a dependable cookie you will stay with over the years.
- *Kittydukonga bars.* Bristling with coconut, this sharp-cornered cookie just wants to jump down your throat. Better the second time around!
- *Raisas.* A sugary potato-marzipan crust encloses a creamy marzipan-potato filling. A cookie the masses can enjoy vicariously.
- *Gracejonesies.* Kind of a mocha . . . no, more like coffee jasmine with a vodka aftertaste . . . or caramel-grapefruit? . . . Not exactly a coating, really, but . . . what is this cookie trying to say, anyway? *Is* it a cookie?
- *Madonn-ahs.* Available by prescription only.

23

They Done Took the Ola! out of Chocolate

A woman called me up at my office one day. She was in a splenetic humor, and she didn't know whom else she could complain to.

I get a goodly number of calls in this category.

This woman had been at the Godiva chocolate boutique in a local shopping mall, where she had seen a glass case full of succulent-looking chocolate morsels with absolutely no indication of their price.

"How much do they cost?" she made bold to ask.

"If you have to ask," the clerk informed her, "you can't afford them."

I doubt that even J. P. Morgan, who is credited with coining that line, could have envisioned the day when it would be applied, with at least a soupçon of accuracy, to chocolates.

You can't say a thing like that to a Connecticut Yankee and expect him or her to take it equably.

You can say it to a New Yorker, and the New Yorker will whip out a wad of tender and bark, "Oh yeah?

Gimme enough of those Gooseberry- and Caviar-Filled Mocha Marzipan Truffles to make me sick!''

If you say it to a Connecticut Yankee, the Yankee will stand there with a strangled look on his or her face and then wander out into the hall, trying, graspingly, to frame a response: "Well . . . I could afford it, maybe, but if it's the kind of place where, when you ask . . . that is . . . in Leviticus we read . . . What am I doing in a mall anyway? I hate malls. I came here to turn in my old kitchen phone, but the phone place isn't here anymore, so I am standing with this old white phone in my hands, noticing for the first time all the marinara stains and finger smudges on it, and suddenly I feel like a *bum* because I'm not the sort of person this boutique sells chocolate to.''

And the Yankee goes home and plugs the phone back in and calls someone, *anyone,* even an author of self-help books, just to have a sympathetic ear. (The Sympathetic Ears, coincidentally, are among the most expensive chocolates in the Godiva collection.)

Reckoning it my duty as a self-help book author, I went to the chocolate boutique to make a full inquiry. The counter person explained to me that it was "company policy" not to post prices. Let the record show that on that day most of the morsels were listing in the twenty-bucks-a-pound range, although they may fluctuate according to the petrodollar or something. The Godiva people would not sell fewer than three morsels a throw, and those would run you around two clams. As far as layaway plans go, there were none to speak of.

I am incapable of paying two dollars for three chocolates, and anyway they would be wasted on my palate, which is just as happy to get a run-of-the-vat Hershey bar as it is to get a designer chocolate Live Starfish and Pesto

Crème Java Swirl. Perhaps happier. And somehow, standing there, I felt like a schnook.

I even thought, fleetingly, about starting my own pennywise line of tough, rigorous, flinty New England chocolates. My father tried something like this years ago. He founded a fictitious company called the Sarah Whitman Hooker Pie Company. Sarah Whitman Hooker was a real-life Revolutionary War heroine who, in the quintessential Yankee version of patriotism, held an English prisoner under arrest in her house for a year and *charged him money* for staying there. Sort of a pen-and-breakfast operation. My father never made any actual pies, never even got beyond the whole business of thinking up amusing names for them, such as Col. Harwood's Sensible Peach for Young Christian Women. (And the obligatory company slogan about trying a Hooker for a change.)

Of course, the old frontier yahoo spirit has gone out of chocolate, not to mention a good many other commodities. Nowadays, chocolate must suffer the dispiriting fate of being rated by *Consumer Reports.* This is true. I was surprised to find *Consumer Reports* delving into a matter so thoroughly governed by personal caprice as chocolate bars. What is ambrosia to one chocolaphage is wormwood to another, but maybe *Consumer Reports* is running out of nuts-and-bolts things to write about. Anyway, there it was, in the November 1986 issue of that splendid magazine: a report on different kinds of chocolate.

CR did what it could to introduce a note of objectivity into the proceedings. It measured such elements as "cocoa mass" and "theobromine" in each chocolate bar. I am not sure what either of those things is or, for that matter, what sort of chocolate-bar consumer would weigh, even for one second, considerations of cocoa mass in his mind while making a purchase.

But after all the figures were toted up, *CR* still felt obliged to enter into the heretofore privileged sanctum of the consumer's mouth.

To that end the magazine published extensive comments on each chocolate bar. The comments were the work of an unnamed "sensory consultant," which sounds like a very odd—and not necessarily desirable—job. Imagine having one's taste buds become a universal standard, like the clock in Greenwich. It could take all the fun out of them. (A fairly small digression: I once had occasion to call the people who are in charge of Greenwich Time. I had become interested in the whole question of whether noon is twelve A.M. or P.M. There is less general agreement on this matter than you might think. Anyway the people in Greenwich were very, very difficult to reach, even factoring in the vagaries of transatlantic communication. I am convinced this is because if it were easy to call Greenwich Time, they would be flooded with calls from upscale jerks arguing about whose Rolex is right.)

Anyway, one reads the sensory consultant's comments with mounting admiration for the man or woman. (Let's say man.) His mouth is an open book to him. Very little goes on in his mouth that he does not know about.

Consider, for example, his comments on the Malliard Eagle Sweet bar: "Relatively bitter. Harsh, woody chocolate, vanilla and fruity notes; too mild. Three or six samples had hammy notes. Too hard to bite; hard chew, slow melt, waxy mouthfeel."

Nice, that "mouthfeel." It's almost a poetic conceit.

> *O mouthfeel, O eyesmell*
> *The tonguesee of Zagnuts*
> *Doth assail my brainfeel.*

You will have noted that the Malliard Eagle Sweet threw the sensory consultant's mouth into a tumult. He experienced, in a chocolate-covered trice, bitterness, wood, fruit, vanilla, chocolate (thank heavens), wax, and ham, or perhaps hamminess. He was reeling from this oral fantasia.

The hammy taste is no lonely aberration. The consultant mentioned hamminess in at least four sets of comments. It makes one think: Should the Sarah Whitman Hooker Chocolate Company capitalize on this quality and actually *go for* the hammy taste, instead of wishing it weren't there? We could put out a chocolate that somehow incorporated the mouthfeel of cloves and pineapple rings.

On the other hand, it may be the case that the enormous pressures of his position have driven the sensory consultant to the unshakeable delusion that someone is sneaking ham into his chocolate.

Still, you have to take your hat off to the consultant who, in noting the inferiority of the Hershey's Krackel to its kinsman, the Hershey's Krackel Big Block, wrote: "Crispies not as evident and less persistent." The persistence of a crispie borders on the ineffable, no?

(A somewhat larger digression: This Big Block stuff reminds me of a problem that I wish *Consumer Reports* would address: the psychic impact of stupid names.

One national doughnut chain, for example, calls its largest cup of coffee The Big One. Some of us in our difficult middle years find it nigh unto impossible to walk into such an establishment and say to a sullen nineteen-year-old counter person, "I'd like The Big One."

So we ask for an extra-large coffee.

"You mean The Big One," comes the reply.

We sigh.

It is somehow even worse than ordering The Big One to be caught skirting, however justifiably, The Big One. One feels prudish. I used to know a woman who could not bring herself to order a Virgin Mary. She would always ask for a Bloody Mary without the vodka. She suffered a similar treatment.

Forget about the place where they sell The Big Gulp. A lot of us won't even go in there. Anyway, *Consumer Reports,* wake up and smell The Big One on this issue.)

Where were we? Ah, chocolate.

At the end of the magazine article, we sense, behind all of the sensory consultant's impressive rhetoric, an unmet longing. He has tasted all these chocolate bars, and their aggregate impact on him has been to make him poignantly aware of the impossibility of attaining the perfection he seeks. He is bloated, depressed, hypoglycemic. On the final bar, he gurgles out only six words, as opposed to his customary profusions: "Unblended flavors. Stale or rancid nuts."

His fingers slip from the keys.

And so do mine.

24

Lost Ann Landers Letter Number Three

DEAR ANN LANDERS: I am a young, attractive, pleasant man who has a nice job and is perfectly normal in every way, except that there is some kind of lemur growing right out of my stomach and I am engaged to marry a 174-year-old woman from a dwarf star and I can't fall asleep at night until a dump truck has dumped at least 380 pounds of loose feldspar—the chunks being no smaller than one and a half inches per facet—onto my prone body. So settle an argument between me and my invisible condor Jim Ed: in Australian-rules football, how many wattles must there be before a murmansk is called? Is it different in the Olympics?

—NORMAL (PERFECTLY) IN BOBO, N.M.

25

Case History: The Baby Who Mistook Herself for Jackie Mason's Love Child

In May of 1988 a judge ruled that the two-and-a-half-year-old child of North Miami actress and playwright Ginger Reiter had been fathered by comic Jackie Mason. In front of a reporter, Reiter asked her daughter Sheba Halley Mason, "How does Daddy go?"

According to the news account, the little girl jabbed a finger in the air and exclaimed, in a Yiddish accent, "How-da-ya-do? How-da-ya-do?"

Since that time we have been monitoring reports of babies who also believe that they are Jackie Mason's love children. Here is the testimony of Corky de la Fontainbleau, one such baby.

My earliest memories are of the womb.

It was a very tough room for a comic, and a lot of babies wouldn't work there. But I learned a lot.

Most evenings I would open with "Good evening, ladies and germs. But seriously, I hope not. I don't have enough problems already with the way this kidney bumps my head? Honestly, people, I don't want to say it's dark in here, but I keep praying she'll swallow a firefly. Hey, these are the jokes, folks. You gotta give a little. I know you're out there; I can hear your Lamaze breathing.

"I wanna be honest with you, things are—is that more ice cream going by? This woman eats more ice cream. Hey, Ma, who's my father, Ben or Jerry?—things are changing. Nine weeks ago I was a chicken. I'm serious. I had a tail. I wasn't worried? What kind of job I'm gonna get with a tail? 'That's my accountant—him with the tail.'

"People, life is different today. Time was, you did nothing. You sat, you waited, you were early, you were late, who knew? Am I right? Now they got this meshuggeneh ultrasound. I hear 'em out there. 'Is it here? Is it there? Is it right side up?' I say, 'Ma, it's got a headache is what! Now get that cockamamy thing outta my ear.'

"Again with the ice cream? Boy, you think I don't get hungry watching all this stuff go by? I tried to order in Chinese. They said they don't deliver. I said, 'Somebody better deliver. What am I gonna do, take driver's ed in here?' Ha-ha. Thank you very much. You've been a wonderful placenta. I gotta go kick for a while, but I'll be back at eleven for the second show."

Birth was another thing. To any young comic wanting to get ahead, I would definitely recommend being born, because the exposure is great. My birth act went something like this:

"Good evening, ladies and gentlemen. I just flew through the canal, and boy are my arms tired! I know it's three A.M. I'm sorry I'm late, but I was meeting with my insurance guy in there. Ha-ha. But seriously, folks, I love the lights out here. What is this, the Sands? Turn it down, Bubby.

"Owwww. Such a knock he gave me. Was that the doctor? It's worse than the ganef in the street. That guy says, 'Give me your money, or I'll hit you.' This guy, he hits you, then he takes all your money. No, no, I would never make fun of doctors. Who makes fun of a guy, he's got forceps on your head?"

"Very lively audience. Is this the delivery room or the morgue? The next time I'm born, I wanna work with a drummer. Thank you and good night, ladies and gentlemen. Thanks so much. You're beautiful."

Then they took me to a room filled with other babies. I would have to say that is the toughest booking I ever had. People crying during your act. I don't recommend it. I developed this material:

"Good evening, ladies and gentlemen. I just wanna say I love this plastic thing they put me in. What is this, a Palmolive commercial? We're going to soak the dishes in this?

"I don't want to say the kid in the next crib is funny-looking, but he already has an offer to open for Berle. It takes all kinds to make a world, and now that this kid is born, I would have to say we got all kinds.

"Okay, okay, okay, shaddup, take it easy. Listen to this girl cry. What is it, they cut up your Discover card? No, calm down. Truthfully I joke. I kid the other babies. We are all the same. Jew, Gentile, black, white, we are all human beings. Except for you in the third row there. I think Marlin Perkins is coming for you. No, I joke. It's not going to be so bad, kid. I hear OSHA is really watching those organ grinders now.

"Oh, look, here comes some relatives to see me. Look at them pressed up against the glass. Hello! Hi! Hello there! Read my lips: you're dummies. Go home. Nice sports coat, Uncle Morty. Did the horse die or is he just out there freezing.

"Ha. I joke. I kid them. I gotta go. Madge the manicurist wants to borrow this tub."

26

What to Do If You Mess Up

Time was, if you had a problem, you just lay still and pained away for a decade or so.

Then, if you had the energy, you might get up and write an anguished poem, book an exorcism, attach leeches, what have you.

And when people messed up on a tragic and mortifying scale, they had the decency to fall on their swords, although I bet that's not as easy as it looks. It's a gesture you would hate—having presumably messed up at something else a few minutes prior—to mess up. Skewer a love handle or something while the opposing forces of King Mortimer laugh their chain mail off. I imagine that back in those days your father might take you out in the backyard one summer evening after dinner and maybe show you roughly how it's done. We don't teach life skills the way we used to.

If you were not too handy with the sword and had an epic sense of yourself, you might even just pitch forward, your heart having burst from the sheer magnitude of your turpitude.

Now, of course, we never get rid of people who mess up.

If *The Scarlet Letter* took place in modern times, Hester and the Reverend Arthur Dimmesdale would appear on talk show after talk show until they had whetted themselves into a kind of telegenic sharpness.

And when we all reached the point where the mere mention of their names caused our Egg McMuffins to stop in their tracts, Hester and Artie would get themselves a 1-900 line and tape rambling, unpersuasive messages with obscure references to church lawyers and numbered accounts—all of it tumbling out into the fathomless depths of telecommunications.

Of course, Hester would be offered a lot of money to pose nude. If you are looking for a doctoral thesis topic in English Lit., ponder the questions of (a) whether she would, (b) if so, for how much money and (c) if so, would she then claim it had brought her closer to God?

It is not enough to be nude anymore either. There are too many nude people around. You have to be nude and famous for something else (having messed up, for example). It is best of all if—from a personal evolution standpoint—you probably shouldn't be nude, but you are.

For instance, *Playgirl* magazine actually offered Paul Volcker a lot of money to pose nude at the time of his retirement from the Fed. He was not an attractive person, but he understood the dollar.

This process exacts a toll from the nude person. Jessica Hahn posed nude and then began—too early in life—to refer to herself in the third person, something you really should not do until you are well into your twilight years and have attained the status of, say, Satchel Paige or Rachel Carson.

Setting nude people aside—as if that were possible—if you have the least bit of a problem nowadays, you are entitled to a television appearance with Phil Donahue, Oprah Winfrey or Sally Jessy Raphael or such others of that ilk as may exist. I don't know that there is any generic name for these shows. They are all more or less committed to examining, over and over, the musical question: Is the General Breakdown in America's Social and Moral Fabric the End of Civilization? Or Are We Loosening Up in a Good Kind of Way, or Is the Breakdown Itself Basically Trumped Up? Or . . .

These shows are getting harder to do.

Back in the old days it was enough to convene a panel of interracial married couples, plus an Outraged Clergyman. Then it had to be interracial lesbian couples, plus the Outraged Clergyman had to have a wooden leg. Then it had to be interracial transsexual professional jai alai players looking to have children through artificial insemination, and the Outraged Clergyman got his leg back, but he had bee-stung lips, and there was something about the way he danced that made you wonder about him.

When they had run through all of those permutations, they did "Children of Outraged Lesbian Clergymen Who . . ." And then their parents, their dentists, etc.

I believe Oprah recently did a segment on people whose lives were so lacking in specific social detail that there has never been a show that spoke to their condition, to the extent that they have one.

Actually Sally Jessy Raphael tapes her show quite near

where I live, which has sparked a whole slew of worries for some of us around here.

The main thing we worry about is whether to call her Sally or Sally Jessy. I mean does the Jessy go with the Sally or with the Raphael or is it pretty much operating on its own in there?

We also worry about whether our little corner of the world will be the kind of petri dish wherein the Sally (Jessy) show can really grow and flourish. We're kind of buttoned down here in Connecticut. I personally know fewer than four transsexual jai alai players, and at least one refuses to talk about it because he's a general in the National Guard.*

So on slow nights, we hang around in front of the 7-Eleven and think up new topics for these shows. Topics such as:

- Women Who Love Just Enough
- Dogs with Multiple Personalities
- People Who Claim They Were Kidnapped by UFOs and Given Bad Haircuts
- Children of People Who Use Apostrophes for No Good Reason (and would, in the preceding phrase, have written "apostrophe's")
- Men Named Brad
- Escapees from Codependent Actuary Cults

---

* NOTE: No, no that's just a joke. In fact, transsexual jai alai players are specifically not allowed to become National Guard generals. Because if they did, the other generals, most of whom are compulsive nude spelunkers, would become nervous. So hundreds of transsexual jai alai players remain stuck at the rank of colonel and . . .

27

Case History: The Compulsive Geraldomaniac

Ever since two Chicago actors revealed that they had faked various problems and syndromes in order to appear on television talk shows, other poseurs have revealed themselves. In this exclusive "Lose Weight Through Great Sex With Celebrities" interview, a talk show crasher recalls her experiences.

I have appeared, under false pretenses, with Geraldo, Donahue, Oprah, Sally Jessy Raphael and on "The Mc-Laughlin Group" talk show.

"The McLaughlin Group" was a real misunderstanding on my part. I didn't know what kind of show it was, and I heard they were planning to discuss why Americans need a lot of sex, so I disguised myself as Morton Kondracke and went on the air. It was the only time I have ever cross-dressed to get on a show. Anyway, it turned out later that they were discussing why America needs a lot of jets, so when I kept agreeing with Pat Buchanan about the difficulty of vertical takeoff, I don't think we meant the same thing.

Oddly enough I think I was on a show with one of those two Chicago actors. Because the news accounts mentioned the impotent-virgin/sex-hating-security-guard episode, and I was on that one, I think. I'm virtually certain. It was Oprah in March '87, right? Or was it Donahue in October '86?

[Sings]

You slept with cheese
You loved too much
Your wife had fleas
You feared the Dutch
Ah yes, I remember it well.

You drop your pants
Your prostate squeaks
You diaper ants
Your Buick speaks
Ah yes, I remember it well.

I wore a snood on Phil
You had a sheep tattoo
Did I make Oprah ill?
Oh no, not you.

I'm a little nervous, talking about this, because I read that Geraldo wants to sue those actors for breaching the integrity of his show. One thing I have come to know about Geraldo is that he is a man of tremendous integrity. He was really decent to me when I was on as a codependent satanic "boomerang phenomenon" daughter who had moved back in with her parents, who knew she (I) was a satanist but didn't know about the accountant part. And then, he was every bit as decent to me when I was on as one of the compulsive dryer-lint chewers.

Here is the thing you need to know: I never planned for this to happen. All I wanted to do was get on one of those shows and promote my book *Inner Peace Through Trout Mockery,* which is kind of autobiographical but has this big section on oil prices, so . . . it's very hard to describe, and none of the shows would have me as a guest.

So I agreed to go on Sally Jessy Raphael for a show about people who have an obsessive need to put Totes products on public statues, and I figured I'll swing the conversations subtly around to my book somehow. But I got kind of caught up in the conversation, because I had tried this a couple of times to get into my part; and, you know, there really is a unique feeling you get putting a rubber boot on the cold stone foot of James Monroe or Lafayette's horse . . . Well, never mind. I got caught up is all.

And I never got around to mentioning my book. So I took another shot at it when Oprah had the show about people who think their teddy bears have carpal-tunnel syndrome. Forget about it. First off, I think it was a mistake to have eight of us on the show, not counting the teddy bears. That's too many people. And the two women in yellow talked so much. You would think their teddys were the only ones in extreme pain. I'm sitting there, doing a slow burn, thinking: Hey, Oprah, how about my teddy bear *who can barely lift its little arms?*

Not that . . . not that . . . I mean, it was just a ruse to get on the show, but . . . I have feelings, just like anybody else.

So I figured I'd try one more shot, and the next thing that came up was a show that Phil was doing about hypertensive personality disorder in gorillas. So I rented a very convincing gorilla suit, and I got on the show, and it turned out that all the other gorillas had trainers or keepers who did all the talking, and it dawned on me that the gorillas weren't expected to say anything, so that's it for my book again.

That's what made me realize I had a disorder—this need to go on talk shows and pretend I had other people's disorders. It's a surprisingly common syndrome and, as soon as they get a name for it, I'm going to be on Mac-Neil-Lehrer.

You know, one of those gorillas had had five bypasses, and it *still* hadn't learned to relax. You could tell.

28

The Prodigal Prostate and
Other Parables

In the quest for self-help, I recently attended a big Health
Expo where one of the booths offered to inventory the
contents of your body for three dollars. I didn't go for it.

For one thing, it seemed to entail the hooking up of
electrodes to one's person, and I prefer to reserve the
hooking up of electrodes to me for more formal occa-
sions: weddings, Michaelmas and so on.

Also, I was somewhat put off when I spotted a sheet of
"How to Hook Up These Electrodes" instructions posted
on a wall for the staff. I prefer to have electrodes hooked
up to me by people for whom it is second nature, if you
follow me.

I'm not a prude about electrodes. I was having some
trouble with my back a while ago, and I would go every
couple of days to the chiropractor's office and get hooked
up to a machine that sent an electrical charge into my
back. I was not surprised by the implication that there was
not enough electricity in my back. I have felt, in general,
that electricity has been leaking out of me, lo, for some

years, possibly through my prostate. My letters to the Trilateral Commission on this matter have gone unanswered.

These treatments made me feel better, but they also whetted my back's appetite for electricity. I would go back to the large, uncaring newspaper where I work, and I would sense my back hungrily contemplating the many pieces of defective and inadequately grounded office equipment, hoping to sidle up to something and get a good, midlevel shock.

And now that this peculiar chapter in my life is over, my back truly misses the good old days of treatments. My back would not be opposed to seeking out some back-alley electrotherapy, where they put you in a hot bath and drop a toaster in. My back has had a rather dull life, and now that it has seen the bright lights of chiropractic, how am I going to keep it down on the farm? This is a big worry for me, especially since all through my adult life, big sections of me have tried to go barreling off in their own directions, with the result that I am often a good deal more akimbo, in general, than I have any intention of being.

For example, my left foot went through a stage of dropping off to sleep for absolutely no reason at all. I began to suspect that it had wandered out of sync with the rest of me, that it had gone nocturnal, that while most of me slept, the foot awakened for darkish podiatric revels best left unthought about.

My chiropractor endeavored to reintroduce these mutinous swatches of me to each other and make them see how important it is that we all pull together as a team.

Anyway, back to this booth—remember the booth? I had other misgivings about having my ingredients analyzed. The booth displayed a sample printout of the body contents of a certain Jane Doe, and it listed Jane's contents as sundry portions of body fat, body lean, body water, body English and body I don't know what else.

It occurred to me that I probably had a better three-dollar opinion of what was inside me than this machine did. No inventory of my body would be complete without:

1. *Necco Wafers* (1.8 percent). Several hundred moons ago, I ate a handful of them, and they failed to bi-odegrade in any significant way. Instead they have turned up in various unhappy crannies of my body in the form of crunchy deposits.

2. *Socks* (2.1 percent). Poets far greater than this rude mechanical of a self-help book writer have written elo-quently of what may or may not cause odd socks to disappear; but I don't believe anyone has ever ex-plored the idea that occasionally the body itself takes a liking to a certain sock and sucks it inside. Once you entertain this notion, however, you can sometimes feel a sock inching around under your shoulder blades or some such place as it continues its ceaseless, sharklike progress through your body.

3. *The Troubles I've Seen* (4 percent). The troubles you've seen leach into your system in the form of small, mouse-colored polyneurons. You will some-times find one lying on the floor near your bed in the morning.

4. *Sock Elastics* (0.2 percent). As if whole socks weren't bad enough, at summer camp I was persuaded that eating the elastics from one's socks was, in some sense, edifying or life-affirming. The proponent of this health practice was (I now see) a peculiar boy named Willie, who ate elastics with a serene, reflective, Bud-

dha-like manner. I don't know what happened to him in later life.

I did try a few other things at the Health Expo. For instance, I sat in a mechanically animated chair that performs shiatsu massage on its occupant by undulating him and kind of scrunching him around. "Shiatsu," it turns out, is what a Japanese person (or almost anyone) says when a machine of this sort locates and breaks a Necco wafer in his back, thus exposing the jagged edges of basic Necco chemical to tender flesh.

But if there was one clear message at the Expo it was: if you want to stay healthy, you have to truckle to a whole bunch of computers. Virtually every booth had some kind of computer in it, but many of the computers did nothing more than the usual sneaky computer trick of restating one's own information in a way that made it sound slightly new.

Hence if you feed lies and preposterous statements into the computer, it will weigh and consider them as sagely as if you had told it something sensible. An example of this sort of exchange would be:

Your name? Googlemush.

How are your feet, Googlemush? Flat.

What is your favorite food, Googlemush? Rutabagas.

How many rutabagas do you eat each week, Googlemush? Forty-eight.

Which of the following substances are you most likely to be exposed to at your job, Googlemush? Plutonium. Shale. Excelsior. Albumen. Actually my name isn't Googlemush. It's Lenny.

Well, Googlemush, our analysis is that someone with such flat feet should eat more than 6.8 rutabagas per day, especially if you are exposed to a lot of actuallymynam. Good health, Googlemush.

This Health Expo appeared to be aimed at a youngish, thirty-five-and-under clientele. I could tell because there was no Prostate Booth. I have been accused of giving too much thought to the prostate, but I don't think any such crime is possible.

For one thing, we thinkers have a lot of catching up to do. Throughout history hardly anyone seems to have given any thought to the prostate. Your Socrates, your Aristotle, your Aquinas, your Shakespeare, even your B. B. King and Muddy Waters have ignored the prostate. And has anything in the world ever screamed out for consideration by the blues more ear-splittingly than the prostate?

> *Talkin' 'bout that prostate o' mine, Lord*
> *Make it hard for me to cross state lines, Lord, Lord,*
> *Lord . . .*

Well, so I am white and not very good on this kind of thing; but where has everybody been on the issue? When my prostate first, as we tend to say, acted up, I took to the bathtub, where I was told I would find some solace. I decided to read *Great Expectations* during these sessions, because I thought Dickens would populate his book with characters whose problems were a lot worse than mine. Instead, with mounting irritation, I found myself noticing that nobody in the whole book—or anywhere in Dickens —or anywhere in Western literature until this very moment—had prostate troubles. Maybe they were called something else. I have always wondered what chilblains, a popular nineteenth-century affliction, could be. Nobody gets them now. Anyway, I also kept dropping the book in the water, and it dried and expanded itself repeatedly until it came to resemble one of those florid, waving sea vegetables.

My prostate, in an act of prodigality, turned on me when I was but a lad of thirty. Let me assure the reader, once that has happened even once, your prostate is never all that far from your thoughts.

It's comparable to when you were little and worried about going to the doctor for a shot. Remember that? The doctor was nice, but there was something about him that made him want to give you a shot. The shot was always a massive, dark cloud blotting out several days immediately preceding your checkup. Will there be a shot? More than one shot? Will it be worse than the last shot? How could it be? The last shot seemed to be nothing more than a syringe full of undiluted pain.

The whole world, in those days preceding checkups, seemed crisply and unfairly divided between those who were in no imminent danger of getting a shot (everyone else) and those who were (you). I don't know about you, but I tended to look with undisguised resentment on everybody who wasn't getting a shot real soon. In the doctor's waiting room, there were tropical fish. Oh, how I longed to join them in those final moments before the executioner's song. To swim, forever circling the eyeless deep-sea diver in those cool, shady waters.

"Try not to think of it so much," my mother would say as I sat there fighting off seizures of fear.

Hah! Tell Marie Antoinette not to think about the guillotine.

As you get older, doctors stop giving you shots quite so often, because it's not quite as much fun for them if you don't mind it much. Still, even in late middle age, you find it hard not to feel a little bit self-congratulatory when you get a shot and take it like a trooper.

Anyway, prostate fear is just a mature form of shot fear.

I was also dismayed to learn that the time of my visit to the Health Expo did not coincide with the presentation of the "puppet show depicting Type A behavior," I saw mentioned in the program. On the other hand, aren't all puppet shows pretty much Type A? What would a Type B puppet show be like? Mellow puppets just kind of dangling around?

That was before scientists released the study saying it wasn't so bad to be Type A after all. I was pretty hacked off about it. All that effort I had put into becoming Type B went right straight down into Roto-Rooter country.

In case you missed out on the whole controversy—which I suppose would be possible if you spent the last twenty years watching Bert Convy game shows or something, you feckless Type B sludge pile—here is how it goes. About twenty years ago scientists said there were two kinds of men, which is what everybody always says, but nobody ever seems to mean the same thing by it.

Type A men, said the scientists, are competitive, uptight, inwardly hostile and worried about wasting time. In other words they have a totally logical reaction to life.

Type B men are . . . I'm not sure what they're like, actually. I don't think I know any. Probably I do, but I haven't noticed them. Type B people, if they exist, are assumed to be more "easygoing," which is to say that they are exactly the sort of shiftless, navel-gazing slackards who can be counted on to gum up the wheels of human progress—if *that* exists.

Way back when they sprang this whole deal on us, the scientists said Type A men were 4.5 times more likely than Type B men to develop heart disease. There has never been a corresponding study of women because even scientists aren't stupid enough to believe there are only two kinds of women or that, even if there were, there would be any way of telling which was which.

Anyway, I worked on being more of a Type B, because frankly my life is very heavily scheduled, and I just don't have time to be having heart attacks. I whipped myself into Type B form in nothing flat.

It was easy, of course, to get my mind to go along with this concept. My mind and I have always enjoyed a cordial relationship. Some of the other parts of me were slower to fall into step.

I might find myself stopped at a long red light, just as calm and Type B-like as you please and perhaps inching forward just a little bit in a very, very Type B-like way, but I would notice my heart racing, despite my mind's strict instructions to the contrary. So I would say to my heart, "What's wrong with you?! *Don't you know what can happen? Are you trying to get us killed?"*

And I found my heart would calm down right away.

In this manner did I become the very model of a modern major Type B person; and then one day the *New England Journal of Medicine* published a study indicating that Type A people more frequently survive heart attacks and may even live longer than Type B people.

Of course they do. The dagblasted, no-account, listless Type B people probably just dawdle right off with the Grim Reaper the first time he shows up. The Type A people say, "Yo, let's see some identification, invoices. You got all the paperwork filled out? Hey, what about all the time I spent in Ohio? You gonna count that as living? All right, then I got some credits coming. And how come my life isn't passing before me? I'm not going if I don't get to see my life. Book a projectionist and get back to me. Also, where's your scythe? What are you, some kinda scab? The real guy couldn't come? Listen . . ."

Anyway, what are we converts supposed to tell our various organs and systems now? That the whole project has been a mockery? Some of our spleens have become interested in Eastern religions. Who knows how they'll take it?

Here is what I think. There should be another type. At least one more. A Type C, which would be very, you know, I'm stepping forward, but I'm not stepping forward; *kum-bi-ya;* if you see Buddha on the road, tell him not to pay a lot for this muffler; I can do that / how am I going to do that? . . .

Well, I don't have it exactly worked out yet, but maybe that's part of it. It *wouldn't* be all that worked out. It would be flexible; and you could be cool, yet still be intense and . . . *C'mon, Mac, it doesn't get any greener than that* . . . very mellow, in a productive sense.

29

Karma 'n' Ghee: A Type-C Memoir

"Are you sure you want to do this?" my wife asked me, for about the eighteenth time.

"*Aruffgn,*" I said, noncommittally.

It was hard to think.

We were sitting in the anteroom of the Golden Eagle Spa in Calistoga, California. Tranquilizing California New Age music by the Lithium Sitar Pacific Orchestra was being piped in, rather too loudly.

Next to me was a California fish tank. It was cylindrical and vertical, like a four-foot-tall coffee thermos, so that the fish tended not to swim so much as hang-glide, catching aquatic thermals upward and then drifting lazily back down.

I wondered briefly about the impact of such an existence on the karma of fish. Did they come to conceive of the universe as one great shaft, and would that make them . . . No, the effort of concentrated thinking about this was just too much for my lotus-leavened consciousness, so

I turned the thought loose to drift on the warm evening breeze.

We were waiting to take the first and only mud bath of our lives. We weren't even sure what a mud bath was, but, as a self-help book author, I felt obligated to investigate any California experience which might bring me closer to the elusive goal of becoming Type C.

The mud baths have something to do with the hot springs in Calistoga, which even has its own geyser. We almost went looking for it until we talked to a guy in the local ice cream-pizza-artichoke-mineral water shop. "It goes off every forty-five minutes, and you wait around, and it's not, ahhh, it's not like Yellowstone or anything," he told us in the dreamy, crystal-cuddling manner of the region.

Anyway, the mud baths have something to do with all that, but it's not clear exactly what, because one doesn't actually bathe in a natural pool of mud. One sits in a big rectangular, coffin-sized tank. And the mud is trucked in. Literally. When we left, we saw a big flatbed unloading sacks of volcanic clay, similar to the sacks of manure and limestone one gets at the garden center.

"What does the mud bath do?" my wife asked the receptionist when we made our appointment.

"Well, it draws out the toxins and leaves your skin feeling rilly soft," she said with a shitake-eating smile.

Hmmphh. I doubted very much that all the toxins I had stored up in all my years of soul-ravaging East Coast newspaperhood could be sucked out into a single batch of volcanic mud. That would be like trying to clean up a major oil spill with one roll of Bounty. I'd probably have to spend about a month inside an actual active volcano before some of the more calcified McNuggets of toxin began to loosen up.

Plus, as our California friend Diane Noomin, a veteran of mud bath action, pointed out, "Not only do you wind up sitting in your own toxins but in the toxins of everybody else who's sat in that mud."

Ooog. Jerry Brown. John Tower. Phyllis Schlafly. There's all kinds of folks I wouldn't care to swap toxins with.

They offered us a special package that included a mud bath and massage, but I drew the line there. I have misgivings about massages. The *Sturm und Drang* of northeastern life has left my body crabbed and pinched in such ingrown ways that I am truly loath to have skilled hands start yanking and pushing and turning loose terrible swift bolts of blinding gestalt-level pain.

Anyway, soon enough we were easing down into tanks of steaming mud.

"It's not that hot," I told my wife.

It got hotter.

And hotter.

"Hrooo," I observed.

After about ten minutes of this, the attendant fetched us out of the mud, had us shower off and directed us into the "mineral Jacuzzi," which was also, in keeping with the theme, hot.

I began to feel as though I had been hot for a very long time, perhaps since the very dawning of the universe, when the primordial gas cloud exploded to form suns and planets and mud and bacteria (which went to live in the mud and wait for me to come along so that it could percolate up through my roasting brain).

Then, just as the steam in my brain was becoming one with the minerals in the Jacuzzi, the attendant got us out and sent us into a little room to lie quietly, wrapped in towels, cooling off and listening to the piped-in Mendo-cino Demerol Oversoul String Ensemble.

Then we left, floating on a cloud of our own mineral-washed unbearable lightness of Type C being.

In the days that followed, I made it a point to replenish my toxins with considerable gusto. And this bunch of tox-ins, by cracky, I am taking with me to my grave.

30

Oh Sweat, Where Is Thy Stink?

Once I spoke to a group of women, and afterward several of them strode up to shake my hand.

The last of these cried out, "His palm is sweaty." This was taken as a sign that I was not as relaxed as I had seemed at the podium.

Well, I . . . I am not going to sit here and make alibis, but I had, in fact, shaken quite a few hands before she got there. Who is to say that someone else hadn't left her sweat on my hand. I'm not saying it was a Donald Segretti-type dirty trick to undermine my credibility, but I'm not saying it wasn't either. Also, in the course of shaking hands, a certain amount of interactive and communal sweat, which is no one's fault in particular, will build up like rain slick on a road.

Still, what if it was my sweat?

I don't like the bad name sweat is getting nowadays. Cooler heads would notice the virtues of sweat.

I admit with good cheer and equanimity: I am a reasonably sweaty person. Most of it (my sweating) is heat-related, but I am not above a little tension sweat.

I am uncomfortable with the direction sweat is taking these days.

Inward.

Sweat should flow out. That is God's and Nature's way.

But there are people who think otherwise, and some of them work for the General Medical Company of West Los Angeles. The company is located on Armacost Avenue, which is vaguely funny. It would be funnier if it were located on Armand Aleggeacost Avenue. But that is a big if. If frogs had wings, the sages have observed, they would not bump their asses on the ground.

The General Medical Company is the proud maker of the Drionic "long-term antiperspirant." Lord, yes. And I suppose the electric chair is a long-term sleep inducer. Because, you see, the Drionic is a battery-powered gizmo that sends electrical currents into one's sweat ducts and kind of zaps them into submission. The shock produces, in the pores, "hyperkeratotic plugs," which the Drionic literature describes (with alarming imprecision) as "not too dissimilar to dead skin."

The Drionic, available by prescription only, has been scientifically tested for use on hands, feet and axillae, which is what scientists call armpits so they won't, when asked about their field at cocktail parties, have to say, "I'm in armpits." (If frogs had wings, would that give them four axillae per frog?)

The Drionic is not, as far as I can tell, intended for use by your average weekend perspirer, although I suppose once it gets whispered around the New York City cotillion circuit, everybody will want one. Mostly it is meant as a boon for persons troubled by excess stress-related sweat.

The Drionic literature asserts that such people often cannot find employment in such fields as electronics and the machine tool industry, where they are unsympathetically referred to as (no kidding) "rusters." (I would expect General Medical Company to be a leader in affirmative action for rusters, although until they perfected the first Drionic, I imagine they couldn't hire any. And even so, pity the poor ruster on his first day of work. "Here's the water cooler. Here's the coffee break area. Here's the time clock. Here's the thing to shock your armpits with. What did you say your name was again?")

The literature does not mention *après*-luncheon women's club speakers, but that may be a whole new market waiting to be tapped and zapped.

"Dermatologists and excess sweaters who have witnessed the Drionic treatment in America and Europe have found it literally a godsend," the Drionic literature proclaims.

Those gods, what will they think of next?

There is something deeply wrong with a world so intolerant of personal seepage that people would choose shock over sweat. You hear tell these days about people who sweat (or do not sweat) the details. It used to be the only thing you could sweat (or not sweat) was sweat. I do not want to sweat details. Details are little gritty brown jagged things, and I do not want them coming out of my pores. Anyway, I am already up to my axillae in details. Why would I want to sweat a bunch more of them?

So I reckon I will stand up and lay claim to the hand sweat found in my possession at the women's luncheon. You get up in front of several hundred women who are all dressed better than you and see if a little something doesn't bead up on you somewhere, no matter how jaunty you appear to be.

The position of this self-help book is that stress has to come out somewhere. And unless you are wiring up a Cruise missile right at the moment, hand sweat is a pretty innocuous form of emission. If you, like a little hyperkeratotic Dutch boy, start plugging up the holes in your personal dike, why, the stress is going to find some other weakened point to come *ploit,* right out of. If it isn't hand sweat, it's hemorrhoids . . . or worse. Just the thought of it has me sweating bullets.

31

Case History: An American Family Describes Its Long Day's Journey into Knight

In today's complex world, more families are turning to intensive therapy programs to help them realize their goals. Perhaps the most controversial program is Knight-spring, in which the famed basketball coach Bobby Knight comes to live with you for a few days and takes charge of your life in order to get it back on the rails. Below is part of the diary of Ambrose Softebrissel of Torrington, Connecticut, who enrolled his family in Knightspring.

MY DAY BEGINS

I churn through the liquid wax of sleep and into the cold hollow of wakefulness. A small dog is on my head.

In our house we wake up surrounded by animals, gazing expectantly at us. For my wife this is not so new an experience. In her halcyon youth, she once lay down in an open field, dozed off, and, hours later, awoke to find herself encircled by an entire herd of cows, all staring worriedly at her, an eerie convergence of the myths of Snow White and Io.

On days when expectant looks are not enough, the small dog gets on my head and executes a step resembling the continental. But today is going to be different.

Today is our first day as a family enrolled in the Knightspring holistic family-enrichment program.

A SUDDEN TURN

"What the blankety-blank is going on here?" Bobby bellows, storming into our bedroom. In his puce bathrobe, his fearsome bulk blots out the dawning sun. "You wake up when I say to wake up. I don't care if the frigging place is on fire and every alarm clock in America is going off, you lie there and sweat it out till you get the go sign from me."

The small dog barks excitedly at Bobby from the soapbox of my head.

"Izzat so?" Bobby roars back. "Well, you got plenty of time to think about it out in the doghouse, because I'm throwing your hairy little white butt out of practice. *Out!*"

The small dog scurries out, and Bobby puts the rest of us through eight walk-throughs of the getting-up drill "until you SOBs know it like Jackson knew the freaking Battles of Bull-freaking-Run!"

A WALK

Now the children have put on their clothes. Bobby stresses the importance of sound, fundamental shoe-tying for children. Our eight-year-old Erskine had gone particularly lax in this department, so Bobby takes him aside and works with him for about forty-five minutes, during which time he calls him a little pussy and reduces him to tears and then helps him find a new reservoir of strength within himself and makes a man out of him and then hugs him and tells him that he (Bobby) would gladly lay down his life for any kid in his program as long as the kid gives 100 percent. Erskine grows tremendously as a person during this workout and will do what is necessary to get his shoes tied properly from now on.

It is time for me to walk the dogs, an area where Bobby feels our program is weak. The dogs like to sniff at horrible things, especially in the spring, when many horrible things long dormant and frozen are beginning to thaw and regain their former piquancy.

But never at the same horrible things. No, one dog pauses to sniff while the other lunges forward; and then it's vice versa, so that my progress down the street is an equilibrium-deprived series of akimbo lurches, shunts and staggers, culminating in the Dance of the Leather Mandala, wherein each dog seizes the other's leash in its mouth and darts around until we are all hopelessly tangled.

"Geeeez," wails Bobby. "You know what you are, Ambrose? A nothing. You're a freakin' jerk. You don't try. You give me nothing. It makes me sick. Really. If I'd had any breakfast, I'd lose it watching you be a friggin' lady with those dogs."

After some hapless drilling, he benches me and substitutes Ed, my neighbor, as the dog walker. Things go much better. Bobby tells me I'll have to play my way back into the lineup. The job is Ed's to lose, for the moment.

BREAKFAST

Bobby will say later that he was unprepared for the shoddiness of our breakfast game.

"The whole freakin' thing here is timing," he fumes at us. "If you got the muffins toasted, but the coffee isn't ready, then where the blank are you? Huh? Huh? Not to mention, you don't take the margarine out right up front, it don't get soft enough to—*hey! pinch the top of the orange juice HARD when you shake it up, you dumb SOB!*"

THE WALLPAPER GUYS

Breakfast takes so long that it runs into the arrival of our wallpaper guys, Joseph and Ray ("like Ray Charles," he always says in his Algerian accent, possibly unaware that this is an unnerving comparison, coming from a wallpaper guy).

Bobby is all over the wallpaper guys like a rash, and pretty soon they both start crying. Bobby doesn't let up.

"You came here to wallpaper, right? Now, I'm going to push you as hard as I can to get some freakin' paper up on this wall that we can all be proud of, you know?"

We all nod. It is only eleven A.M. We are just a few hours into our Knightspring training, and already some of the gauzy, dreamy, indistinct contours of our lives are beginning to acquire sharpness and definition.

We wonder how we ever settled for the numbing mediocrity of our past life, and we vow in our hearts to turn our program around.

We will take responsibility for what is wrong with us. We will become better people. We feel we owe it—if not to ourselves, then at least to Bobby.

32

What's Wellness Without Sickness?

There are loads of self-help books purporting to tell you how to be healthy, but how many of them bother to instruct you in the sweet science of being sick?

Not many, Bunky.

I'm not talking about how to *get* sick, although that is not as easy as you might think, especially when you are desperate to be sick. In fifth grade Tom Tribuzio and I were in such grave trouble with school authorities that we really felt we could no longer attend school. Our only hope, we believed, was to develop some kind of lingering, consumptive nineteenth-century illness. Tom reported some prior success with the technique of licking his bathroom floor, a veritable Serengeti plain for your major bacteria.

As I said, we were desperate. So we did it. All I can tell you is don't try this at home. Don't even try this at Tom Tribuzio's home. Actually the real tragedy in this story is not so much that we licked Tom Tribuzio's bathroom floor but that, having licked it, we failed to get sick.

At least not right away. I have had occasion to wonder whether some recurring neurological difficulties that have persisted well into my adult life and subsequent dotage are the result of licking Tom Tribuzio's bathroom floor.

Anyway, that is not the point of this chapter. What is the point of this chapter? Probably I would remember if I had not licked Tom Tribuzio's bathroom floor. Let us say that the point of this chapter is what to do when, having presumably licked something or other that you shouldn't have, you get sick.

The first and toughest lesson of being sick is: don't go into work. This is a delicate subject. People who think they are needed at work fall into the same category of people who look at photographs of themselves and cry, "Oh, what an awful picture of me," while the rest of us stand around tugging our forelocks and wondering what to do with the awkward knowledge that, no, the photograph is pretty much right on the money.

Very few people are truly needed at work. Magic Johnson. Gunther Gebel-Williams. A couple others. Everybody else, starting with Lee Iacocca and ranging on down through Paul Harvey and Orville Redenbacher, and ranging down even further through the President of the United States and the Pope and then plummeting right down to you, everybody else is not really needed at work on any given day.

If the Pope is out for a couple of weeks, maybe somebody from Catholicism stops by with a few vouchers for incense and indulgences needing his signature, but that's about it.

Nobody loves those people who drag their swine-flu-infested bodies into the office with the light of industrious bravery glistening in their bacteria-glazed eyes. They are the Norway rats of the workaday world, carrying plague to all corners of the American business spectrum. Far from contributing anything by their presence, they actually create extra work by dint of their feverish moiling.

Life is tough enough without getting memos and phone calls of this sort:

> To: Bob
> From: Ray
> Re: Diebolt Grommet Recast
> We have to ream out the Vancouver office on the subject of inventory asparagus mmmmffffgl' FLAHG FLAHG spiders on my flesh. THUD.''

The recipient of such a memo will invariably waste valuable work hours trudging down the hall to discover the sick colleague sprawled across his or her desktop making little spring frog noises into the Dictaphone.

So don't do us any favors. Go home, huddle under blankets, and let the spores war it out across the Argonne Forest of your flesh.

It can be a wonderful time for you. When you're lying abed with very little to do except feel the peculiar jolts of mutant-spiked viruses careening wildly through your metabolism and glancing off your inflamed lymph nodes, you have an opportunity to give some careful thought to your own personal philosophy and perhaps crystallize some new insights that have been lying, pooled up over the hair-clogged drain of your soul.

Spend some time developing a creed. (Creeds, by the way, will be in during the nineties. People in singles bars will be asking, "What's your creed?" and so forth. So get a running start.) Your creed might be, for instance, that you would prefer in the future, if it's not too much to ask, for someone other than you to get the flu. Even if four or five people had to get the flu in order to exempt you, you might consider that a reasonable arrangement.

The risk of cogitating when you're sick is that you may get a great idea—a terrific new plot line for "Dagwood" that you long to scratch out and mail overnight express to whoever draws the strip. You can't act on any of your ideas when you're sick. All you can do is lie there and issue unreasonable demands like the French child-kings of the watchamacallit era.

Who were those child-kings, anyway? You're too sick to look them up.

"Honey, could you look up who those French child-kings were? Also, get me a ginger ale?" Try that one out on your spouse.

It is a terrible thing, to be so dependent on anyone. When your spouse prepares to leave the house for the day, you will be tempted to groan out a few bars of "Ruby (Don't Take Your Love to Town)." Don't do this. Your spouse will keep going right out the door, and then it will be just you and Kenny Rogers alone in the dead, viral air of the house.

Unless you have a dog. Dogs don't understand being sick. They think you are experimenting with the notion of becoming a dog. They hunker down enthusiastically like counselors at a scientology weekend. "I told you it was great! Lie on the floor panting. Sleep. Spit up once in a while. You'll love it! Here, have some pine needles."

When you get over the flu, you generally need another day or two to recover from ginger ale poisoning. Sickness creates, in human beings, the need for ginger ale. Even before ginger ale existed, the very first humans tore apart all the naturally carbonated springs in the Indus Valley looking for something that resembled ginger ale when they got sick.

During times of wellness, five or six cans of ginger ale might be enough to get you through the whole year. With the flu, you knock back fourteen liters of the stuff and still the very sputum-coated membranes of your karma vibrate with a yearning for more. It would probably make sense to have a Schweppes tank truck pull up to the side of your sick room and pump the stuff in.

Your system is not ready to absorb a ginger ale tsunami. Your system is ready for two, maybe three of the things which crash against it over the course of a year, and ginger ale toxicity is not one of those things. There should be something comparable to the Betty Ford Clinic for these cases. Maybe it could be named for the little winged lady on the White Rock bottles, if anyone knows her name.

The only other succor available to the ill is videocassettes. It is not at all clear what sick people did before the Age of Videocassettes. Suffered and died is my guess. Videocassettes heal. If there had been videocassettes around at the Crimean War, things might have gone differently. I'm not even sure about how things actually did go, but I believe that if there had been videocassettes, Florence Nightingale would have cut more of a Crazy Eddie-ish figure.

While you are in the deepest throes of your illness, you will probably be dependent on a spouse or other loved one to go to the store and rent videos for you. You must pray that this trusted person in your life does not suffer from Videocassette Rental Concentration Impairment (VRCI), a crippling disease which strikes one in seven Americans.

I am married to a VRCI sufferer. My wife walks into a video rental outlet, and some kind of *petit mal* seizure sweeps over her. It is difficult to say what happens next, but she leaves with two videos that invariably, somehow, represent a less canny selection than she could have made by playing a video rental version of Pin the Tail on the Donkey. A good deal of the time, the donkey is Donald Sutherland. I have nothing but respect for this fine Canadian actor, but he turns out to have snuck off and made several dozen low-budget Italian movies about men who believe they are tapirs and while away their days gazing out rain-streaked hotel windows and wondering what they should do next.

And it is no good asking my wife to seek the counsel of Big Al, an upstanding local high school student and video rental store employee. Big Al's teachers have done their best to instill within him an appreciation of Faulkner and Kipling and Milton, but none of this has served to make him a keen judge of cinema. Big Al's only contribution to my convalescence has been to see to it that I am as familiar with the work of Kiefer Sutherland as I am with that of Kiefer's father.

The consequence is that until I am strong enough to rise from my pallet and make the arduous journey to the store and exercise my constitutional right as a mature, thinking adult to rent a movie in which Lisa Bonet dances seminude with a chicken, I must lie still fantasizing about what sorts of movies Milton would have authored had he lived in this age.

Or I can watch daytime broadcast television. Daytime television is tricky. It can worsen some conditions. There are several facts you should know before you watch it:

1. The old FCC rule requiring that "Barney Miller" be playing on at least one cable channel every minute of the day has been rescinded and replaced by a similar one applying to "Mork and Mindy."

2. There are, inexplicably, hardly any good cartoons on television during the week. Most of them tend to be these product-related sagas involving characters with pharmaceutical-sounding names such as Darvon and Lomotil.

3. Beware of apocalyptic television documentaries. You are in no shape for them.

One day, when my wife was home with a cold, I came back to find her in a state of terror because of a television documentary she had seen about Nostradamus, a sixteenth-century French seer who predicted a whole series of calamities, pestilences, floods, droughts and multifarious unhappinesses. (This was back in the time when seers had to emphasize that sort of thing because there wasn't an audience for the truly gripping psychic predictions one encounters today, i.e., *UFOs will make Linda Evans marry William "the Refrigerator" Perry.*)

A lot of Nostradamus's calls, according to my wife, have already paid off at the cashier's window of history. But in just a very short time, my wife explained, the Wheatena was really going to hit the chainsaw. I'm not sure what we are supposed to do about all this. Maybe take out a second mortgage, blow it all on Dom Pérignon and then head for high ground.

You can hardly blame a sick person. After a day of watching daytime television, any of us would find it plausible that someone—probably someone with good taste—is going to rain fire and pestilence on humankind.

I am as amenable to such notions as the next person. So I rushed out and acquired a couple of books about Nostradamus. Actually one of them combined the prophecies of Nostradamus, St. Malachi, the Great Pyramid at Giza, Edgar Cayce, Jeane Dixon, Arthur Treacher, Ambrose the Penguin Boy and Reginald Pfister the Finder of Expired Self-Dates. Some of those, anyway. The conclusion? A chunk of Halley's Comet was going to whang into Earth and tilt the planet's axis, setting off a string of horrific events that would make you wish you lived in Fargo, South Dakota, which would probably be a major seaport by the time things settled down.

I took this book out to the park with me on my lunch hour and read it under a tree. By the time I stopped, I was actually getting a little misty-eyed over all these poor innocent, happy chumps eating hot dogs and throwing Frisbees out in the June sunshine, soon to be swallowed up in flame-gargling chasms.

And what about me? I was on the verge of becoming an acclaimed self-help book writer. Just as I reached for the gold ring, I was to be flooded and plagued and marched upon by the Antichrist. Can you stand it? Isn't that just the way it always works out?

I certainly don't pooh-pooh this stuff, mainly because it may come true, in which case you would be grabbing my lapels (if there are still lapels) and screaming in my face, *"And you said it was all a big joke!"*

Hmmm. We seem to have wandered away from the subject. Do you see? This is the sort of thing that has been happening to me ever since I licked the Tribuzio bathroom floor.

33

Why I Don't Live Where You Live (and Vice Versa)

One of the greatest sources of modern malaise is the gradual estrangement of people from their own dwelling places.

For example, it has occurred to me that our house is very dry during the winter. I am not the kind of person who can grab hold of such an idea right away. The idea has to waft and loop through the air around me like a paper airplane. We are going on three years in our current house, and it has finally sunk in that our house is dry.

I am a good instrument for measuring humidity. When I am dry, I begin to flake apart, like mica. When I am moist, I am like a Duncan Hines cake.

Not everyone is like me. You just look at Alexander Haig, and you know that he is always dry to the spiritual core, no matter how damp the world around him happens to become. The karma of Diane Sawyer, on the other hand, is probably always moist. These two people are not at the mercy of their surroundings, and I envy them that.

It must be nice to be the captain of one's own personal dew point.

My life in our house resembles, somewhat, those promotional sponges that plumbers and other tradespersons used to hand out when I was a kid. I haven't seen one in a while, but the sponges were flat when you got them. Immersed in water, they would expand in a way that provided a mild form of excitement.

I have tried immersing myself in water when I am dry, but it doesn't work.

One of the disadvantages of being dry is that it somehow obliges you to assume a greater share of the world's electricity. When I come home at night, great bolts of mad-scientist lightning leap up to greet me. I don't know why this should be so. If I had known that force fields were going to take such a personal interest in me, I would have paid more attention in science class. I will hazard the guess that electricity is like hair, in the sense that if you wet it down, it lies flat and doesn't make so much trouble.

After I have been walking around the house receiving shocks to my dry lunar surface, I can look down by my feet and see traces of a fine powder. The powder is Basic Colin McEnroe Material that has precipitated from the Colin McEnroe Mother Ship.

One Jekyllish self-help experiment I have considered involves gathering up this powder over time and mixing up a kind of Carnation Instant Breakfast of myself. Then I would glug it down and perhaps become more myself than I currently am. You could think of it as Colin McEnroe Helper. Maybe I would appear to have more density and depth.

The perspicacious reader will wonder why my wife and I have not bought a humidifier.

We have given thought to this very subject, but when we go to the store, we see only ultrasonic humidifiers. (Ultrasound, like lasers, will be creeping steadily into our lives in the next decade. Most of our toasters and alarm clocks and facial sauna machines and coffee makers will be powered by one or both of these dimly understood forces.) We looked up ultrasonic humidifiers in *Consumer Reports,* a publication we keep on hand to remind us that almost any step we take to improve our lives will result in an intensification of our misery. *Consumer Reports* tells us that ultrasonic humidifiers can make your life vastly worse, if your water is hard. Our water, I'm told, is very hard. I don't know what this means, but my wife does (so I don't have to—that's what marriage is all about). I have rapped on the surface of our water and it seems about average.

I'm not sure what happens when you add ultrasonic steam from hard water to a dry house full of bodies electric. When *Consumer Reports* begins to describe the potential for dire calamity that lies behind most everyday activities, my hands tremble, my vision blurs, and I have to go lie quietly for a while.

Anyway, if I get too dry, I can always go out and sit in my car. Our small dog, Mildred, has the habit of licking the windows on my car. A strange kind of damp vapor has built up in there, and there is no getting it out. It moves around, from surface to surface, often without much warning, pushed by unseen intra-Toyota trade winds.

One moment it's on the side windows, and the next it has come rushing like a Canadian air mass toward the front of the car. There is a capricious terrier-spit weather system in my Tercel. I keep waiting for it to assume the form of some important religious figure, but it never does.

If there is some kind of device that will transfer cumulus dog breath humidity into a dry house full of hard water and mildly electrocuted people without using ultrasound, I would like to know about it, I guess.

Otherwise, I think I can live with things the way they are.

That's often the best course. People spend way too much time nowadays trying to create artificial environments in their homes rather than live with what Fate handed them.

I went to one of those home shows, and I saw so many unnatural products that I wondered what Edgar Guest would have written had he lived today.

It takes a heap o' livin' in a house t' make it home,
A heap o' built-in saunas and a geodesic dome,
It takes a fiberglass Jacuzzi and a nice acrylic spa
And a sunlamp and a hot tub, t' make it Shangri-la.

Judging from the home show, American society is headed into the tank. There were so many whirlpools, spas, hot tubs, Jacuzzis and sundry other Charybdises that you felt kind of stupid about going home and standing under your measly little shower.

"What is the meaning of all this?" I asked a guy presiding over a fleet of sloshing spas and whirlpools (which, as near as I can figure, are pretty much the same thing, in home show parlance). "Why does mankind suddenly feel this need to immerse itself in warm, moving water?"

"Stress maintenance," he said.

"What does *that* mean?"

"They get a little hyped up, so they get in there," he managed, with some neurological effort, to say.

The goal of human life, apparently, is to become one vast mangrove swamp.

Softness, that's what it is. I'd like an enterprising young historian to check out some fallen empires and de-stroyed civilizations—Rome, Babylon, Duluth, that kind of thing—with an eye to how much time was spent lying around in warm water. First sign of a culture gone slack, I'll bet.

Spas, saunas, ultraviolet rays. It was heartening to en-counter the booth of the Gutter Man. In these sybaritic times, at least there is still one sturdy soul willing to hun-ker down with something as nitty-gritty as gutters.

> *Beside the frothing Jacuzzi*
> *The village gutter man stands;*
> *A mighty man is he*
> *With large and sinewy hands.*

"I don't wanna buy, Stella," a peevish man snarled at his mate as they passed me by. "I just wanna get some ideas. Because our home is not *comfortable* to me."

You see? It's all comfort and softness. (They even had soft toilet seats on display.) In Edgar Guest's old poem, a house is not fully a home until the angel of Death has passed through it and claimed a loved one. You think anyone will put up with that in these pampered times?

"I'm not *comfortable* in here, Stella. Someone *died* in the sauna. It's *creepy*. It's *gross.*"

The coming thing, I am given to understand, is smart houses, operated by computers.

> *Our house*
> *Is a very, very, very smart house*

With 285K RAM
Life used to be a sham
Now everything is friendly 'cause of use

The idea is that houses can be electronically programmed to look after themselves and to talk to their owners. You could call up your smart house from work and tell it to warm up the hot tub for you. You could tell your smart house to start the ultrasonic toast and laser coffee at 6:28 and wake you up at 6:28:30. You could tell your smart house to keep an eye on you and call the authorities if, after watching "The McLaughlin Group," you went into a state of total paralysis.

Whether your house would do any of these things would depend on how smart it was and what kind of relationship you had with it.

My house, for instance, is pretty stupid. If I asked it to make me some coffee, it would probably just sit there wondering what to do until big tears of frustration rolled down its walls, creating a mildew problem, which I would have to do something about before I could have some coffee. I would probably wind up having to make *it* some coffee. At least it wouldn't be so dry around here.

On the other hand, I get along with my house okay. Not great, mind you. It does not wag its chimney at me when I come home, but I don't insist on that. The house is keenly aware that it was once owned by doctors and that it has indisputably come down in the world.

Mainly, I don't want to get too emotionally involved in my house's intelligence. I would just hate running into people at the supermarket and having them say, "I hear your house has to stay back this year."

Or having them ask, "How did your house do on the boards?"

On the other hand, it would be nice to have a slightly more communicative house. Occasionally I sense that my house is pining away in some fashion to which it cannot give words. Or perhaps it is trying to alert me to some impending catastrophe, the way Lassie used to try to tell uncomprehending humans that Gramps had just been sucked into the compost heap.

"What's wrong, girl?" I will ask my house, but it merely creaks plaintively. Later, a hairball the size of Kohoutek erupts from some aperture of the plumbing.

My plumber Pete seemed to be able to discourse with my house. He had a closer relationship with the house than I have with the house or than he had with me. He called me Tom. At least, he called someone Tom. The only entities present when he was speaking were me and the plumbing.

"It might work, Tom; it just might work," he would say, softly, doubtfully, while contemplating some wild and drastic measure.

He may have been talking to the plumbing itself. I don't doubt that, alone in the darkling netherworld of the basement, plumbers whisper to the plumbing in its own secret language of sighs, gurgles and clanks. But Tom? I think the plumbing has a name more arcane and stranger to the human tongue than Tom.

Pete eventually retired, if not from plumbing as a whole, at least from our house and its plumbing. He became increasingly sullen and made little sotto voce remarks which implied that we had secretly installed bits of cubist or postmodern plumbing in our house for no other purpose than to confound him.

With Pete out of the picture, I confronted the possibility that I might have to work on my house. I advise readers of this book against undertaking any difficult home repair projects, a category which embraces, basically, all home repair projects.

There are two reasons to avoid these projects:

- They require skill.
- They require effort.
- They require a lot of difficult figuring with numbers.

Shortly after we bought our current home, I noticed that the door to one room did not close all the way. After several days of complex calculations, I determined that this was because the door was somewhat larger than the doorway.

I went to the basement and fetched a plane, one of the many useful tools my father gave me as a cruel practical joke. I rubbed the door with the plane for several hours in such a way as to have no impact whatsoever on the problem. I rubbed much harder, with the result that a large portion of the door came away. So the door closes just fine now, mainly because there is enough space between the door and jamb for a large Australian fruit bat to fly through without missing a wingbeat.

This phenomenon is not confined to the actual structure of one's house. I recently determined that my refrigerator was not working, by removing various things from it over a period of days and pressing them to my forehead. The fact that none of them was the least bit cold tipped me off. Also, I thought I recognized a number of liquids that, in happier times, had been solids.

My first panicked thought was to call Pete, but a consultation with several reference books persuaded me that a refrigerator isn't, in the strictest technical sense, plumbing.

My second thought was to inspect the back of the refrigerator, where the main workings of the device are situated. A refrigerator runs by converting the dust behind it into a peculiar mutant, reptilian substance. There was plenty of that stuff behind my refrigerator, and it was not on fire, so I determined that I would have to call a repairperson.

This is not as simple as it sounds. Many repairpersons are themselves estranged from their very livelihoods. Often a refrigerator repairman, when reached by phone, will seem almost annoyed to have been pestered about something so trivial as a broken refrigerator.

We suffer from the additional burden of our other dog, Roy, who regards any repairperson who might visit our home as a potential member of an international cartel of dog food thieves. Consequently, many repairpersons offer shady and implausible explanations of why they cannot come to our house.

"I don't fix refrigerators no more. I'm a urologist now."

"Not unless your dog tells me what he did with my pickup truck."

That kind of thing.

Eventually we located a repairperson who had never heard of us or our dog. He lived many hours away, up near the Canadian border, so it took him a while to get here.

When he arrived, after a brief inspection he told us the problem was that there was ice in the freezer compartment.

See, this is a perfect example of a fundamental misconception by a layperson. I would have thought that ice in the freezer compartment was pretty much a natural—even ideal—state of affairs. You get ice forming on the shower curtain or under the coils of your electric range, then you've got a problem.

Anyway, the ice was removed for the mere approximate cost of completing the Aswan Dam, and the repairman began his long journey home. I removed several jars and vegetables and pressed them against my forehead. The normal order of things had been restored.

My advice to anyone facing a crisis of this kind in the future is to contact my neighbor Ed immediately. Right about the time Pete was overcome with plumbing ennui, Ed moved into our neighborhood. If Ed were given the opportunity to run America, you would be surprised at the number of things that were in shipshape by the end of that period. At the very least, he should be choppered in to all major catastrophes such as earthquakes and the Grammy Awards.

Ed has a need to fix things. Sometimes, if we see him coming up our driveway and there is nothing particularly broken in our house, we take a sledgehammer and whack some complex-looking device just so he won't be disappointed.

So it was that we turned to Ed when we had a problem recently with our hot water heater.

My philosophy is to remain in a state as close to total ignorance about the goings-on in my house as I can possibly achieve. I didn't even know we had a hot water tank. I thought the pipes ran directly from our faucet to some great steaming, bubbling caldron in the Utah salt flats. For years the hot water tank had sat mutely in a dingy corner of our basement, wrapped in padded white bunting. I had come to think of it, dimly, as some kind of enormous, featureless stuffed toy or commemorative statue of Ziggy, the bloblike cocktail napkin personality.

Anyway, our hot water tank abruptly lost interest in containing hot water and turned our basement into a miracle oozing-statue-of-Ziggy-at-Lourdes grotto shrine. When the water continued to deepen, my wife and I faced the fact that our prayers to Pat Robertson for a spontaneous tank healing had gone unanswered.

Ed turned up and told us to go get a new hot water tank at Sears. I had never gone to Sears to purchase something as big and intrinsically life-affirming as a hot water tank. It made me feel like a rugged Sam Shepard backcountry type.

"While we're in town, let's us have lunch at the *ho*-tel," I told my wife, tugging at the bill of a workingman's cap I had dug out of some far corner of the closet for the occasion.

At Sears, we were attended by a salesperson relatively unencumbered by specific knowledge about hot water heaters. She did, however, know about recent insidious changes in American consumerism. I'm not sure when this started, but it does seem that nowadays all major purchases are divided into two steps:

Step 1: You tell the salesperson you would like to purchase said item.

Step 2: The salesperson asks if you would also like to purchase one of several "plans," representing various levels and intervals of enthusiasm for fixing the product. The dilemma is: Do you merely want the product, or do you also want some psychic reassurance that you can count on it for longer than three months?

(Optional Step 3: Cybernetic telephone voices call you up and hound you to purchase extensions every time one of these service plans expires, so that, little by little, your washing machine approaches the approximate sticker price of the Goodyear Blimp.)

Anyway, we somehow got a hot water tank and hauled it back to our lagoon, where Ed installed it while I offered to call an EPA containment squad or an exorcist or Bill Moyers every time water came gushing out of something.

But Ed knows all kinds of tricks, such as using Wonder bread to stop up leaking pipes while he's working (which proved utterly ingenious, but every once in a while, for a day or two, I would turn on the faucet and a small abominable gobbet of Wonder bread would leap out at me).

If I had a smart house, I suppose it would never let matters reach such critical stages. There are smart houses which can independently summon a repairman when they sense something going wrong.

This would never do for me. My house seems to enjoy its time spent with people like Ed and Pete a good deal more than its time with me. It would be forever trumping up hypochondriac excuses to invite them over.

This could put me in a difficult position with various repairmen.

"What's this bill for rewiring? I didn't ask for that."

"But, sir, your house insisted . . ."

And who knows who else the house would call.

"Listen, house, the phone bill indicates that you've been having long conversations with a condo in Tulsa. What do you guys talk about, anyway? Your operations?"

There are smart houses whose owners can phone them and ask what the temperature is in the basement. This is doubtless a great comfort to those owners who know what the basement temperature should be. I would wind up with a worrywart smart house which would nag me about all kinds of things I don't understand.

"It's forty-seven Celsius in the basement. Whaddaya wanna do, boss?"

"I don't know. Is that bad? Can you call the McCarthy house and ask it what the temperature is in its basement?"

An educated house would put on airs, and I would feel foolish yelling, "That may be the way they talk at house school, but as long as you're under my roof . . ."

34

Case History: A Man and His Missile

More and more homeowners, confused and frightened by détente, are making the personal choice to own missiles. Although this book does not take any position on the highly charged subject of federal missile control legislation, we have granted space to a missile owner, who wishes to remain anonymous and probably would if he weren't so plainly Gervaise Pugh of Burnt Umber, Missouri, so that he may explain his choice. The following is his tape-recorded testimony.

I wasn't raised to be a missile owner. My parents did not have missiles. As far as I know, they never even owned a bazooka or grenade launcher, and I doubt they do today. Frankly, I've kind of lost touch with them. In this man's world, it's tough enough looking after your own defense needs without having to look after a couple of namby-pamby secular humanists who never, in all your wonder years, lifted a finger to keep you out of the hands of Communist agitators.

No, I didn't come from a missile background. They had always frightened me a little. I had never even fired a missile, believe it or not.

And I don't want you thinking I got my missile because of a few "weirdos" in my neighborhood. I'm no alarmist. I've always considered my machine guns and attack dogs and mines and viper traps and recombinant DNA death mung to be all the deterrence I'll ever need against weirdos. In fact, I'm getting rid of the dogs because, if it comes down to it, I don't want anyone saying, "He let his dogs do his fighting for him."

No, I got my missile because I felt just plain uneasy. Every darn night I turn on the tube, and there's that buttonhead Brokaw yammering about the Straights of Vermouth or whatever, and you know perfectly well that when the scat hits the air conditioner, he and his type will scuttle down into their underground honeycombs where they'll sit out the action breeding a whole new race of hot-combed, Voltaire-reading nancy boys, while Average Joes like you and me duel it out with Ivan and his Sandinista flunkies.

Still, the typical reaction I get is: You don't need a missile to defend your property. That's what police are for.

What these people don't understand is that, on my property, late at night, *I am the police. I am Eliot Freaking Ness and Batman and Robin. Okay?*

I'm sorry. I got a little het up there. I believe I merely grazed you. Here's a little peroxide. Tape recorder didn't take a hit, did it?

As a first-time missile buyer, I had only the usual ballpark notion about what I wanted: quick-reaction firepower, inertial guidance, terminally guided reentry, affordability, smooth handling and handsome styling. I found a little number from Martin Marietta that won my heart with its rich Corinthian leather-padded console.

I also signed up for a missile safety course, where you actually go out to the Bikini Atoll and fire a few times, just to get over the apprehension you have about firing a missile. When the time comes, I don't want to wind up giving myself a hot foot while the bad guys get away.

The other important thing was to make sure that the kids understood that the missile was not a toy. So I called all the kids together and said, "Kids, the missile is not a toy. Under no circumstances are you to play with it. How do you think I would feel if you all blew yourselves to kingdom come and, when the Ayatollah showed up in my driveway, I had no missile, just because of the irresponsible actions of a bunch of little house apes?"

Anyway, when I get up at night and look at my sleeping family and then gaze out at the missile with its blinking control lights, I realize that what I really bought was peace. Peace of mind. My mind.

But I'm not going to act like I know all the answers. I admit, it is absolutely true that I fired my missile, by mistake, just once, at Burlington, Vermont.

The thing is, see, I was having a dream where Vermont declared war on us, and I must have gotten kind of semiawake and launched the missile at them, and I'm real sorry about that.

On the other hand, the civil defense folks up there got some much needed practice in.

Did you know that the mayor of Burlington is a Socialist? I'm not saying that excuses anything, but . . .

35

Lost Ann Landers Letter Number Four

DEAR ANN LANDERS: My wife, she, you know? She don't . . . A man's gotta right, you know? But . . . my wife, she don't. Ah, what the hey, it's a free country, eh? Sign me

—WELL, IS IT OR ISN'T IT? LITITZ, PA.

36

Getting Too Rich

Many purchasers of self-help books are grappling with a creeping, leaden feeling that life is passing them by, that they may be little more than a poorly installed Molly bolt holding up life's rich tapestry, as opposed to being actually visible on life's rich tapestry.

Why, these purchasers ask, am I not a glittering presence? Why do I not have an ostentatiously large and tastelessly furnished house full of sullen hangers-on?

Such worries are nothing new. Decades ago, Jung noticed that many of his patients experienced a keen absence of luster and sheen from their lives. He eventually concluded that they felt a profound sense of loss at not having been Cybill Shepherd. (True, Cybill Shepherd did not actually exist at that time, but it was already clear to Jung that somebody was going to get to be her.)

Anyway, I want readers of this book to have the kinds of lives they deserve. So as kind of a parting gift, as you near the last pages, I am offering, exclusively to you, the chance to get in on the ground floor of Dr. McEnroe's

Dinosaur Air Products, which will be my contribution to the new American practice of building ragtag armies of people recruiting other people to sell dubious products that nobody wants, such as fly pollen enemas.

These dinosaur air products are based on the discovery —which I read about in the *New York Times,* so I know it is true—that the dinosaurs breathed air that was 50 percent richer in oxygen than the crummy stuff we are stuck with nowadays.

Scientists were able to extract and test some 80-million-year-old air bubbles trapped in chunks of amber. The *New York Times* did not mention it, but I am sure they pulled these bubbles out with tentative jerks. I mean, if you have ever encountered the air bubble surrounding, say, four-month-old cream of zucchini soup in a Tupperware container in the back of your fridge, you know that air bubbles do not always age that well.

Anyway, this dinosaur air, fetched out of amber found in northern Manitoba, showed oxygen levels as high as 32 percent. The earth's air currently contains about 21 percent oxygen (although the oxygen content in Connecticut, where I live, is better represented by those little asterisks they use on cereal boxes to indicate that any riboflavin you might happen to find in Praline-Mallow Monster Flakes would have to be the result of an accidental chemical spill).

Some experts have contended—not that I want to alarm anyone—that if the atmospheric oxygen level gets much over 30 percent, the entire planet, or at least Morton Downey, Jr., would burst into flame.

So my plan is to buy up as much of this old amber as I can get my hands on, although I would feel better about the whole prospect if I were a little more sure about what amber actually is. I believe amber is sort of the geological equivalent of what happens when someone passes you a box of assorted chocolates and you bite into something that turns out to be abominable and you don't know what to do with the rest of it, so you slip it into your pocket and forget about it and then discover, many days later, this highly unpleasant little nodule where the bottom of your pocket used to be.

Anyway, I will extract the dinosaur air with tentative jerks and package it somehow, probably in those air horns ordinarily filled with freon, so that people can just stick the business end up to their mouths or ears or wherever they feel they need a good jolt of dinosaur air and blast away at themselves.

Then I will recruit a whole bunch of tentative jerks to sell this product, which I figure will be popular because people are very keen on dinosaurs right now, despite the fact that they were, near as I can tell, shiftless, low-life, no-account animals who neglected their health.

Eventually I will have assembled a vast pyramid of aimless capitalist enterprise in which so many people are entitled to a cut of the action that no one could get rich off it, even if the product we sold was the staff of life (which is Parmesan cheese, by the way). Actually, I'm trying to figure out how the preceding sentence differs from the American economy at large—without much success, I might add.

So if you're interested, read on. (Obviously, if you are already Cybill Shepherd, you can skip the whole thing. And probably have.) I was going to try to include, in each copy of this book, some of those reply cards that come fluttering out of every publication you open these days, but then I decided there are limits to how annoying even I am prepared to be. I have actually had a disturbing dream in which I break through a cave wall near Nag Hammadi

and discover urns full of ancient Coptic scrolls. As I unfurl
the first scroll, a subscription card to some Gnostic exercise magazine flutters out.

Anyway, instead, I am including the following shame-
less advertisement.

Dear Reader,

People used to make fun of me. "Ha-ha," they
said. "You are just a lowly self-help book author with a
messy desk and a wart on your foot."

I was down to my last nickel when I chanced to
meet a millionaire who confided in me: "Since you are
a nice fellow and seem to be willing to listen and perhaps even loosen your grip on my windpipe, I will tell
you **a wealth secret known only to the rich and
powerful.**"

He did, and it started the wheels turning in my
head. "Aauugh aroog," I cried. "How do I make
these wheels stop turning?" But he had fled out of the
alley.

Now I am rich and own **imported European cars**
which are **imported** and **loaded** and have **telephones**
and are considered **imports** and a **fancy penthouse** at
the top of a **building** with **furnishings.** Attractive
nurses inject me with **monkey gland extracts** so that I
will **live forever.**

If you're ready for a change in your trifling viral
existence and would like to be **rich** and own cars that
are **imported** with **one owner** and **low mileage** and
some (imported) rust, clip and mail in this coupon:

Dear Colin,

Yes! I am ready for a change in my dismal and

sebaceous life. I want to be rich and have friends like Bob Hope and Brooke Shields and frequently lapse into boldfaced type for no apparent reason. Here is $15 so that one of us may realize his dream.

37

Case History: What Color Is Your Phone Booth?

A psychiatrist from the city of Metropolis submitted this report in 1988, right around the time a well-known pop culture icon turned fifty.

S. first came to me with complaints of sleeplessness. "I don't care who you are; when your prostate goes, it goes," he said sourly.

He also claimed that his clothes were too tight and that his home—which he bitterly described as the "Fortress of Solitude"—had acquired a musty odor "like old penguin guts."

S. had just turned fifty. He had never married, was sexually naïve, had no hobbies and little grasp of the concept of recreation. He had spent all of his adult life fighting, in his words, "a never-ending battle for truth, justice and the American way."

It had made him a terrible bore. So much so that even the other superheroes made excuses to avoid him.

"For about a year, I never got the mailings for the Justice League of America meetings. They said it was a computer foul-up, but I don't know . . . Even that green guy who hasn't had his own comic book for decades gets the mailings. Reminds me, did I ever tell you about the time I fought the huge robot that Brainiac made out of gamma particles and how I fused the air around it with my heat vis . . ."

I appear to have dozed off somewhere in here, for when I awoke, S. was no longer in the room.

In the early sessions, S. talked extensively of his feelings of rejection by his biological parents, who allegedly put him in a rocket ship when their planet blew up.

"How do I know any of that's true?" he agonized. "How do I know they're not living in a retirement community west of Tucson?"

Unable to work through any of his Oedipal drives with the saintly Ma Kent, he had displaced some of his sexual energies onto the task of saving humanity. He also admitted, however, to some fetishistic feelings about the *Daily Planet* building and, in April 1965, had a vividly homosexual dream about Jimmy Olsen for which, twenty-three years later, he continued to feel guilty.

"His signal watch was beeping, and, and, oh, I can't talk about it," he fretted. "You know, there was another time, though, when the archfiend Metallo put kryptonite in some paneling I was installing, and I had to use my super speed to . . ."

My notes become somewhat hazy at this point, because of a fugue state into which I appear to have lapsed. S. was not there when I came to, and, perhaps significantly, his check for that session (written against an account at the First Bank of the Bizarro Planet) bounced.

In the subsequent sessions, I encouraged S. to explore

his feelings toward Lois Lane. He claimed at first that she was just a "nice girl."

It seemed significant to me that a man of his sort would pick, as his primary love object, a woman who—for all of her professions of undying love—so often appeared to be manipulative, scheming, devious and spiteful.

Could it be that a relationship with such a shallow and disingenuous woman would allow him, in a safer context, to project some of the anger and resentment he felt toward his own mother?

S. veered off abruptly into a lengthy and extremely tedious anecdote involving himself, Lex Luthor, a red sun and the Phantom Zone. I dropped into a hypnotic state almost instantly.

After more than three years, a breakthrough occurred. S. had attempted to spend a week on Guadeloupe with Batman, Robin, Wonder Woman and the Green Lantern. Things had not gone well. S. would not be specific. Apparently, though, Batman, Robin and Wonder Woman have a very unusual arrangement.

S. wept disconsolately and complained, "All the women I ever meet are screwballs or have gills or something."

He admitted for the first time that he hated saving mankind and that he had begun to suspect mankind of deliberately getting itself into fixes just to deprive him of any opportunity for leisure and happiness.

Treatment continued for a year after that. At this time, S. has left superheroing altogether. He has moved to Seattle, where he operates the Daily Plankton, a macrobiotic restaurant.

I have not been there, but word has reached me that the broccoli and blue-green algae empanadas are outstanding.

38

What to Do in the Supermarket, Part Three

What else binds us together, as a race, in the supermarket line? The magazines arrayed before us like bright pennants round an Arthurian pavilion.

The tabloid people have calculated that, there in line, blocked by carts fore and aft and perhaps reconsidering our choice of ice cream, we experience sufficient softening in the hardware of our consciousnesses to allow consideration of statements such as JILTED FORT WAYNE MAN SAYS: HITLER REALLY A WOMAN.

I have always felt that the tabloids play an underappreciated community mental health role. It comforts us to know that Princess Diana runs the same risk of becoming pregnant from freak heat lightning phenomena as anyone else.

Which is why this self-help book writer is worried.

If a recent page 1 of the *New York Times* is to be believed—and I don't see why it should be, inasmuch as all of its EDITORS ARE SPACE ALIENS—supermarket tabloids are toning down their sensationalism.

The *Times*—a newspaper whose PUBLISHER ADMITS: I FATHERED 300 DEVIL BABIES—also claimed that the market for these fine weekly publications is going soft and that circulation is dropping, which can only mean that STUPID PEOPLE ARE INEXPLICABLY DISAPPEARING IN DROVES.

I have divided feelings about this new development because the GHOST OF SEBASTIAN CABOT CONTROLS RIGHT SIDE OF MY BRAIN.

I have always enjoyed supermarket tabloids. If you could get past your stodgy, old-fashioned notions about the truth, you would find that tabloids are more imaginative and, in general, more apt to contain lively writing than most would-be legitimate newspapers or, for that matter, this book, its title notwithstanding.

My main gripe with the tabloids, however, has always been their attitude toward the afterlife. My careful reading of their articles over the years has revealed to me that when you die, you (1) meet Elvis, (2) meet all of your relatives, (3) meet all of Elvis's relatives, (4) learn from Marilyn Monroe the cure for arthritis, (5) meet with a couple of Elvis's aunts who couldn't get free to see you when you first arrived, (6) get, from some angels, a diet that allows people to eat unlimited numbers of Hostess Pudding Cakes and still lose weight, (7) meet Elvis again because he forgot to give you your hospitality fruit basket. And so forth.

I dunno. I was kind of hoping the afterlife wouldn't be quite so Type A. I was hoping I would get a chance to unwind.

My other gripe involves Bigfoot. Bigfoot formerly cut a figure of considerable dash and pluck, when you heard about him only once in a while, but the tabloids have really beaten him into the ground. He has become the crypto-zoological equivalent of Bob Uecker, in the sense that the things we once liked about him annoy us now.

The tabloids should develop a bigger palette of dubious monsters from which to choose, including:

1. The Viper-Goose of Delaware
2. Oogi, Half Puma/Half Maître D'
3. Jack Kemp

But no, it's Bigfoot, Bigfoot, Bigfoot. That's the real problem with the tabloids—narrowcasting. They assume that we readers carry rather slim briefcases of enthusiasms. They assume that upon arrival in the afterlife, the first thing we will all want to do is meet Elvis. This may be true in some cases,* but many of us will have a bunch of other names on our dance cards.

Publications in general have tended to narrow their focuses in the last decade or so. I notice there is now a magazine for women over forty. I feel odd about that. Sort of the way you feel when the people at the table next to yours in a restaurant ask to be reseated somewhere else. Were we making them uncomfortable, or . . .

Why do women over forty need to go off in a corner and huddle by themselves? What's the big secret? Hot flashes? Hey, *I* get hot flashes. Probably Bigfoot does, too.

* In the South, one will encounter, in public places, paintings on black velvet of Elvis shaking hands with Jesus. My wife has often remarked upon the way older Southern women like to sing and talk about Jesus as though he were almost a romantic figure, a secret lover with whom one walks and whispers, at whiles, in perfumed gardens. The sacred is made slightly erotic. Now along comes Elvis, who started out being erotic and, in death, appears to grow more divine by the day. Is this some dimly understood attempt to bridge the eternal chasm between the sublime and the profane? I have no idea, but it is the only remotely scholarly proposition in this whole book. I will probably come to rue ever touching upon another of my wife's ideas. In my last book, I mentioned her theory that Snoopy is popular because he resembles a breast, and it was virtually the only thing the reviewers quoted.

So right there we have a common bond that will go unrecognized if our periodicals Balkanize us.

More and more, I find myself slouched at the newsstand looking for just a, you know, general kind of magazine, but there aren't any. Instead, there's *Slouch: The Magazine of Enervated Carriage.* Instead, there's *Naïve: The Magazine for People Who Cling to a Starved Notion of Unity.*

I don't want to be part of a subgroup. I want to be part of the vast, burbling flow of humankind. I don't see why John Simon, Ti-Grace Atkinson, Kareem Abdul-Jabbar and I couldn't all read the same magazine.

The last time I knowingly read a magazine pitched at a special-interest group, it was something called, I believe, *Highlights.* It was a children's magazine. Everybody read it, but nobody I have ever talked to can remember anything about what was in it.

This may be because we usually read it in the waiting rooms of doctors and dentists, where we were too paralyzed with fear to concentrate properly. Wave some rubbing alcohol or Novocain under our noses, and we'd probably have total Proustian recall.

Actually, I can remember one *Highlights* feature: "Goofus and Gallant." They were two hypothetical children—one ill-bred, the other noble. Each month, a particular disparity in their approaches to life would be duly noted, e.g., "Goofus strikes wooden matches on the sides of other children's heads. Gallant never plays with fire."

Here is the irony: Goofus, of course, grew up to be Carl Icahn or some other successful person. Gallant is running fund drives for public television. Even we kids could not fail to notice that Goofus got top billing, mostly because only his behavior was interesting. (Any tabloids listening out there? You could dig up a great scoop if you could locate these people. GALLANT: I KEPT A CYCLOPS LOVE SLAVE.)

Geez. What else was in that magazine? *Highlights* Forum? "I used to think all those letters in *Highlights* Forum were made up, until the other day I was greasing my bicycle chain and these two brownies came over to ask me . . ." No.

The message of today's print media is: Here's a magazine about people just like you. Ugh. Who wants to read about people just like oneself? That's why I don't watch "thirtysomething." I *am* thirtysomething. I need to know more about self-involved white guys?

I guess that if I don't want to read a magazine about myself, I could read *Self,* which is, one assumes, a magazine about the sort of people who do want to read about themselves. Why is that logic unsettling to me?

Or I could read tabloids, which are never about oneself, unless one is Elvis, Bigfoot or Princess Diana.

What if tabloids were about oneself? Perhaps that is what is meant by "toning down sensationalism." Perhaps the tabloids mean to include more stories of humdrummery.

DULL SELF-HELP BOOK AUTHOR SAYS: "SATANIST HYPERTRICHOLOGY CULT OWNS MY LOVE HANDLES."

It would never sell.

39

Lost Ann Landers Letter Number Five

DEAR ANN LANDERS: I'm not one to pry, and I'm not one to tell other people how to raise their children, and I'm not one to go where I'm not wanted, and I'm not one to show up at weddings of people I don't know and hurl frozen turkey giblets at the bridal party, and I'm not one to paint faces on coconuts and arrange them around the living room and turn on loud music and scream "Party down!" at them.

But I do all these things anyway. What do you make of it?

—NOT ONE TO ASK

40

Case History: A Gorilla Who Loves Too Much

The following two actual news items appeared in newspapers around the United States in the spring of 1988:

WOODSIDE, CALIF., April 3 — Koko, the celebrated signing gorilla, spent a half-hour Saturday with actor William Shatner, better known as Capt. James T. Kirk of "Star Trek."

WOODSIDE, CALIF., April 4 — Koko, the Woodside gorilla who gained international recognition through her use of sign language, has issued a pressing message: She wants to have a baby.

The circumstances under which the following correspondence was obtained prohibit us from commenting further.

Dear Bill: How you? I fine. Weather good. I burn with love for you. You have baby with Koko? New life forms. New civilizations. Boldly go. You the best. I miss you. Still smell Paco Rabanne after-shave in

cage. We be great team. Like Bob and Libby Dole.
Critics never give "T. J. Hooker" fair shot. This just
one gorilla opinion. Sorry this letter so messy. Ante-
lope drool on it.

                    Hugs,
                    Koko
KTG:pp

Dear Mr. Koko: Thanks for your letter. I regret
that I cannot send each of my fans a personal reply
when they write, but the sheer volume of mail makes
that impossible. Rest assured, however, that I'm
"beaming" with enjoyment of the letters you folks
write. I hope to see you at some future "Star Trek"
event. And now, warp factor seven, Mr. Sulu!

                    Your friend,
                    William Shatner

Dear Bill: Hey what is deal? I get form letter from
you. Koko melt with love for you. Maybe you call
Koko? No wait bad idea Koko no talk. Bill you take
Koko to animal research prom. You ask soon. Panda
name Shane hitting on Koko in big way. Koko hold
him off for while. Koko no want to be seen with guy
who eats bamboo. Koko see you last night on box.
You go to planet where everybody made of Lycra or
something. You kiss lady wear enough eyeshadow to
cover Ivory Coast. Then she turn you into purple ter-
mite nest. Singles scene no good for you Bill. You
better off with Koko.

                    Hugs,
                    You know who
KTG:pp

Dear Koko: I'm so sorry about the mix-up with the first letter. But really, this is the wrong time for me to get involved in a long-term relationship with a gorilla. There are grave challenges facing Star Fleet Command in the coming days. Plus, my agent has pretty much nailed down a deal for me to do a national tour in *Amadeus*. It's down to me and Larry Storch anyway, so . . . I'm not sure you understand any of this. But try to forget me.

Bill

Dear Bill: Boy long distance love not so cheap now that stamps a quarter. What this country come to? Can't wait till Gephardt get in White House. Anyway now you back away, huh? Koko hear about guys like you on Oprah. Commitmentphobes. Ugh. You read *Smart Gorillas/Bad Choices*? That story of Koko's life. Saw you last night on planet with big hairy white lobsters. You kiss different lady. She pretend not know what she doing. Then she try suck brain out your ear. (Saw same lady on "Murder, She Wrote." She older than you think. Anyway Martin Landau kill her. No wait maybe James Franciscus. Why he not get better parts now?) Single scene too violent Bill. You need settle down.

Hugs,
Your little banana breath

KTG:pp

Dear Koko: There are some things we need to straighten out. I'll fly out this weekend, and we'll talk.

Bill

Dear Bill: Never mind fly out. Koko try let you down easy. Koko meet nice gorilla at mixer last night. His father in movies. Tight with showbiz crowd. Personal friend Irwin Allen. Go lots parties. You find someone else nice Bill. What Connie Stevens up to these days?

Thanks for memories,
Koko

KTG:pp

P.S. Saw new next generation star trek program. Bunch yuppies. You still the best Bill.

41

Don't Change a Thing

Perhaps it is fitting that we end this self-help book with the newest movement in pop therapy—the sameness movement. Perhaps it is not so fitting. In any case, we have run out of paper, so when this is over, turn in your headsets and make your way quietly toward the exits. (It should be noted that some archdruids of sameness object to the term "movement," since the word runs so contrary to their goals.)

Daytime talk show host Gottlieb LaHook brought world attention to sameness programs when he enrolled in one and displayed the startling results on his own show.

Here is a transcript of LaHook's remarks on that history-making broadcast:

First of all, you should know that it took a lot of guts for me to come before you and talk about this, because of everything that has happened.

But I decided to do it for all of you out there who have

tried all the stay-the-same programs that have come along in the past and have found that you just couldn't stick with them. I have found a medically supervised program that works for me, and for the past two months—here, take a good look now, people—I have stayed exactly the same.

Thank you. Thanks so much. Really. Your applause is the greatest compliment I could have gotten. It means more than all the glowing magazine articles about me or the insistence of many famous artists and photographers and decoupagists that I become the subject of their next great work.

I know it's tough to stay the same. Nobody knows this better. I have had a change problem, really, since I was a kid.

Some of it is behavioral. My mother was constantly shoving change at me. Feel a little blue? Get a new haircut. Nothing to do? Here, affect a new mannerism. Anxious? Go on a diet. Lonely? Take up yoga.

I don't blame her for this. She comes from an ethnic culture—we're Nauga-Etruscans. Yes! Thank you. Some other Nauga-Etruscans out there—an ethnic culture where change was a typical way for a mother to show love and concern.

Our society, too, subliminally encourages change. From the time you're little, you get rewarded for it. Hey, he can walk. Great. Hey, he can use a pencil now. Good. Hey, he stopped eating ants. Terrific. Is it any wonder, with this kind of reinforcement, that so many of us grow up to be change junkies?

As I got older . . . well, I don't have to tell you folks. You've all watched me go on one crash sameness program after another. The Grapefruit Consistency Regimen. Hypno-alikeness. One and the Same. Sit Tight to Win! Analogousness Through Crystals.

All of them worked for the first few weeks. The real problem was keeping change off over the long haul. And you folks who've been through this know that the temptations are all around us. Everywhere you go these days, the subtle inducements are there: Quit your job, get married, move to the country, join a cult, get cosmetic neurosurgery, whatever.

I'd be out in public, sticking right with my unvarying routine, and I'd see somebody across the room enjoying some . . . change. And I'd think, boy, does that look good. Boom, like that, I'd be gone, stuffing myself with difference and variety and adjustment.

Anyway, I want you all to know that I found a program that works for me, and I've stayed exactly the same for two months!

Thank you. That means so much to me. Although it does not affect me in any lasting sense.

I also wanted to lay to rest all the rumors. Yup, I've seen the tabloids. So: no, I haven't had the lobosuction; no, I haven't had the adrenal gland transfusions from Dick Clark; no, I haven't had the bionic gyroscopic stabilizer implants they gave Fred MacMurray.

All I have done is enroll in this Stable-Tech Behavior Nonmodification Program. Now, I have to say, it's not for everyone. I'm the first to point out that not all of you can afford the $75,000 a month that a media person like me can pony up.

For me, it works. Wherever I am, three times a day, my man Friday Y'aboud ties me down and gives me the injection, and that's all there is to it.

The greatest thing is the reactions I get from all the people who haven't seen me in a while. They don't always spot it right away, so at first they'll just look at me kind of funny.

Then they'll say, "Have you . . . Is there something
. . . kind of indistinguishable about you from the way
you were? Especially given the fact that, over time, we all
. . . shift a bit?"

"Yes, I've lost a lot of change," I'll murmur.

"It's probably in the seat cushions. Ha ha. Get it?"
they'll say. Yeah, like I haven't heard that one a million
times lately. These jerks think they're real comedians.

Still, it gives me a huge rush.

Not that it influences me in any intrinsic way. I mean,
not that there are any . . . consequences or . . . ramifi-
cations that have a bearing, in any way, on who I am.

And even if there were, I don't see how just a little
teeny-weeny bit of . . . almost invisible . . . evolving
could do a person any irreparable harm.

What am I saying?

Thank you for coming to my side right then and pointing that out to me. I *was* weakening. Bless you all. Thank
you for supporting me. I love you all.

Stick-in-the-muds.

FREQUENTLY USED PHONE NUMBERS

Police _____

Fire _____

Water _____

Earth _____

Richard Gere _____

Your Imaginary Friend _____